# 101
# OBAMA
# BLOGS

## By

## Will Clark

# 101
# Obama
# Blogs

Copyright© 2013 by Will Clark

ISBN 10: 1492210188
ISBN 13: 978-1492210184

Published by
Motivation Basics
P.O. Box 6327
Diamondhead, MS 39525
Will01@aol.com

For more information about the author
visit
AuthorsDen.com

# QUOTE

"A nation can survive its fools, and even the ambitious. But it cannot survive treason from within. An enemy at the gates is less formidable, for he is known and carries his banner openly. But the traitor moves amongst those within the gate freely, his sly whispers rustling through all the alleys, heard in the very halls of government itself. For the traitor appears not a traitor; he speaks in accents familiar to his victims, and he wears their face and their arguments, he appeals to the baseness that lies deep in the hearts of all men. He rots the soul of a nation, he works secretly and unknown in the night to undermine the pillars of the city, he infects the body politic so that it can no longer resist. A murderer is less to fear. The traitor is the plague." Marcus Tullius Cicero, 58 B.C. Speech in the Roman Senate

# INTRODUCTION

Barack Hussein Obama began his presidential campaign with a promise to 'share the wealth' of the country and to 'spread the wealth around.' He never once promised to create an environment in America to help the poor earn their share of the wealth. His was a promise to give them something, not to give them the opportunity to earn something for themselves by being part of productive society. He promised the poor a free dole.

His initial action was to create class warfare by separating the consciousness of American society. He labeled their enemy as the 'millionaires and billionaires' so their target would have a classification and could be identified. He would be their savior to make those millionaires and billionaires share their wealth with them. They believed him and they followed him. Many even worshiped him as a deity. They became his 'doles.' His doles will follow anywhere he leads them, even into places alien to the visions of our Founding Fathers.

Obama has used the same practices and techniques as did Vladimir Lenin in Russia and Adolph Hitler in Germany to create loyal followers. He told his doles what they wanted to hear - and he became powerful. Lenin convinced the proletariat, George Orwell's proles, the ruling class was their enemy. His proles helped him destroy a once proud Russia. Jewish merchants were Hitler's target. He convinced poor Germans they were keeping Germans from being successful, and they followed Hitler to destroy Germany's once great nation.

The 101 blogs in this writing are taken from those I posted on my site at Authorsden during the past two years. In combination, they reveal my belief that Barack Obama is a danger to the survival of our great country, the United States of America, similar to the danger created by Lenin and Hitler. His, however, is more insidious and cunning.

# 1

# A King Rises

What would be the most likely scenario for a president (specifically Barack Obama) to actually take over a country and begin autocratic rule. Recently, after all the research for my new book, 'King Obama: America's Greatest Danger,' I've discovered it would be simple, especially with our increasing emphasis on security.

That process might begin with many small terrorist attacks inside the United States. This would allow the president to proclaim 'martial law.' In fact, the public might even demand it. What might initiate this activity? An article by Kristin Tate of mrconservative.com, June, 2013 gives a good clue:

"It is usually assumed that most illegals caught crossing the US/Mexican border are South Americans. You may be surprised to learn, however, that thousands of the illegals caught crossing the borders are classified as "OTMs" (Other Than Mexicans). A substantial number of these OTMs are Muslim terrorists. Records from a detention center near Phoenix, AZ, show illegals from Afghanistan, Egypt, Iran, Iraq, Pakistan, Sudan, and Yemen in custody. Former Arizona Congressman JD Hayworth said in an interview, "There are definitely people out there who mean to do us harm who have crossed that border."

A Congressional report shows how most Muslims are illegally entering the country. They travel from Europe to the tri-border region of South America. While there, many of them learn to speak Spanish, and then blend in with Mexicans attempting to enter the US.

In another report, WSB-TV 2 published a population breakdown from an Immigration and Customs Enforcement staging facility in Florence, Ariz., dated April 15, 2010, which includes detainees from as far away as Afghanistan, Armenia, Bosnia, Egypt, Ghana, Iraq, Iran, Jordan, Kenya, Morocco, Pakistan, Sudan, Uzbekistan, Yemen, Botswana, Turkey and many other countries. Based on U.S. Border Patrol statistics, there were 30,147 OTMs apprehended in fiscal year 2003; 44,614 in fiscal year 2004; 165,178 in fiscal year 2005; and 108,025 in fiscal year 2006. Most were caught along the U.S. Southwest border.

According to the Department of Homeland Security's 2008 Yearbook of Immigration Studies, from the Office of Immigration Statistics, federal law enforcement agencies detained 791,568 deportable aliens in fiscal year 2008 – and 5,506 of them were from 14 "special-interest countries." The State Department lists the following as "special-interest countries": Afghanistan, Algeria, Iraq, Lebanon, Libya, Nigeria, Pakistan, Saudi Arabia, Somalia and Yemen."

In summary, there are enough Islamic terrorists already in the U.S. to create much havoc - when the right time is determined. But what about high-powered weapons? Where are those weapons lost during 'Operation Fast and Furious?' Were they really lost? And, unknown to most - there were other 'gunrunning' operations taking place at the same time - and with the same results; many lost weapons.

Recent revelations about the new NSA programs

provide the other part of the picture - unregistered weapons owned by U.S. citizens. If a president orders martial law, he would most certainly order confiscation of all weapons from armed citizens. But, there is no national registry of citizen arms - right? Wrong. The massive capability at the NSA center will allow instant information about any weapon or ammunition purchase anywhere in the country. Other than with cash, any purchase gives a trail to the type of weapon, the person's name, and address.

And, with a cashless society, very possible in near future, our government will know where you are, what you are doing, what you have bought, and what you own. By cross-referencing property registrations, auto registrations, gasoline purchases, and many other sources and items - Big Brother will know more about us than we will know about ourselves. There will be no secrets by anyone - except those who have cash. Those who have cash at that time might even be considered 'terrorists' and eliminated with a little shot from a passing drone.

There are many ways for a despot to take over America. The simplest, however, is to have martial law with a cashless society. My current book, 'America 20XX: The New World Order' details these possibilities.

# 2

# The Doles

A special program will be on Fox News tonight (August 9, 2013) giving details of food stamp abuse, and maybe even fraud. But, I guess the government is so anxious to get more people on food stamps that the idea of 'fraud' is not a consideration. If Obama's administration wants more people to get food stamps then why would they investigate anyone not eligible to get them for the possibility of fraud. If anyone who simply asks for them gets them, then there is no qualification process. I wonder who has to pay for all those food stamps that would be fraudulent if fraud were a consideration? Perhaps the taxpayers?

The same concept applies for obamaphones. Phone companies get paid for the phones they distribute to 'needy' people. According to several surveys - and braggadocios on TV news programs, many people have two or three free obamaphones. Some even have an obamaphone as a spare stand-by in case the one they paid for themselves has a problem. I wonder who are paying for all these 'needy' obamaphones? Perhaps the taxpayers - or in the case of obamaphones - other cell phone users.

Why are these questions important? When Obama began his campaign he said he was going to 'spread the wealth around' and wanted everyone to have their 'fair share.' Perhaps two or three obamaphones and food stamps to everyone could be considered a 'fair share.' Or it could be considered a fair dole to everyone. I went to wikipedia for the definition of dole. It was: "allotted share, portion, or destiny, a giving or distribution of food, money, or clothing to the needy, a grant of government funds to the unemployed, something distributed at intervals to the needy; a 'handout' something portioned out bit by bit."

Perhaps for the true needy these handouts could be considered valid. In the old days it would have been considered the 'Christian' thing to do, and was often managed by Christian churches. But since Obama said the United States is 'no longer a Christian nation,' perhaps he wants to discourage their benevolence. Perhaps now Obama considers it a 'dole.' instead of the 'Christian' thing to do. And, since Obama's purpose for handing out the 'fair share' is to use the dole for that purpose, then perhaps the recipients of those un-needed fair shares should be considered 'Doles.'

George Orwell in his book, '1984' had his 'proles' that were controlled for their votes. It seems Obama has his 'Doles' that are controlled for their votes. Don't forget - they are 'Doles,' promised their fair share.

# 3

# Proles and Doles

While editing and re-formatting my new book, 'King Obama: America's Greatest Danger,' for the Kindle version, I realized an erroneous analogy I had made. I guess it's not really an error - probably just a cultural interpretation. Anyway, I gave this different view in the Kindle version. It's regarding George Orwell's use of the word 'proles' in his Big Brother book, '1984.' Applying the idea of 'proles' within the Obama realm left a big question every time I did that edit. I finally realized what was missing and made the correction in the Kindle version, which is now available. This excerpt from the book below gives that correction regarding the concept of 'proles' and 'doles.'

"Every president before Obama struggled to show America as a shining example to the rest of the world, even during times when the country struggled for mere existence and survival. Perhaps all were not totally successful, but the welfare and progress of the United States were the ideals that guided their path and their decisions. Obama's torch seems to light his path to a different direction for the future of America. His doesn't seem to be focused in the same direction as all other American presidents before him. Shouldn't the safety of citizens and the freedom to develop to their highest and best be the highest concerns for any president or leader? He divides the country by rhetoric and deeds, criticizing those who have been blessed by our great nation to achieve higher levels of prosperity and success. That's the success necessary to offer ladders to others to achieve even more success for themselves. Without successful people with enough to invest in opportunities for others America would not be the shining star of the world. Obama's actions have been to extinguish that opportunity ladder by penalizing those who reach those success levels. He uses magnificent rhetoric to extol his virtues as an economic genius and leader who will help those at the bottom rise to middle-class, while at the same time he kicks the ladder of success from beneath them so they can remain at the bottom. They remain at the bottom with no place to go except to the government to beg for more welfare and direct assistance.

Perhaps his great followers and worshipers are not really 'proles' after all, for 'proletariat' suggests a working class. Perhaps those who worship him and wait for his promised handouts instead of working for their 'fair share' should be identified as his 'Doles.' Doles could be described as that large body of people waiting for their fair share, their dole, to be portioned to them bit by bit. Getting their 'dole' does not erroneously suggest they are making any effort to earn it by being part of the working class - the proletariat."

It's his doles who give Obama his greatest support. They are the ones who wait for his handout instead of being among those who contribute to our great nation.

# 4

# Obama Distractions

Its' back to my true writing love - fiction and education subjects. I just realized at the end of July that most of my sales were two fiction books and an education book.

During the past year, I got seriously distracted trying to alert readers to the dangers of our government. There are two problems with writing about serious government topics, especially with enough information to develop an entire book. First, it takes a lot of research and cross-referencing - and that consumes a lot of time. (My golf game has gone to H—, you know where.) Secondly, the information changes daily. For instance, I heard on news this morning that Congressional members and workers are now trying to find a way to exclude themselves from Obama's new health care system. That tempts me to write more - but there will be a new revelation tomorrow - and tomorrow - and so on. Anyway, as I researched for my recent work, I learned that there is already enough information on the internet to alert everyone of our government danger.

I started another novel before I got distracted trying to 'save the world.' (It took me a while to realize that most are not interested or don't really care - or are afraid to have their names connected with anything the government could use against them later. Anything now on the internet can be monitored, including their names and what they researched.) I got 8,000 words into the novel. 'From Troy to Ephesus,' before I got distracted. Anyway, I'm back to that and will probably change the title to something without defining and limiting the ending - maybe carry it all the way to our current government events.

My two recent novels are associated with government events in fictional format. Although they are stories, it's clear what's implied by reference. Those two are: 'America 20XX: The New World Order', and '666: Mark of the Beast.' These are serious current theme novels. Of course, I have several others that I wrote just for fun.

My education books are also gaining more interest now. I guess that's because the new school season will be starting soon.

Okay, enough of this distraction. It's back to 'Troy,' or the golf course. Troy can wait another day!

# 5

# A Foundation

A president, any president, any leader has the responsibility to bring all people together in a common cause for a country. Barack Obama has failed miserably in accomplishing this task. He hasn't even tried. In fact, he has contributed to the racial divide.

To bring the racial divide together two things are key - and he has failed at both. First is education. To get a job, ordinarily one must be educated to the level of a job requirement.

When he became president, the first thing he did was to appoint the least qualified education leader in America to be the secretary of education. Was Obama's destruction of the education system intentional, or was he doing a favor to one of his Chicago buddies?

At least 50-percent of black children never graduate effectively from high school. Many who do are not 'educated.' Are Obama and Arne Duncan not astute enough to realize that those who can't compete in a classroom must still be educated to qualify for a job - other than selling drugs on street corners, and committing burglary? Can't they understand that many kids who do these things want a job - and would do well in realistic job-training programs. Job training programs must replace many of our standard high school academic programs - or this generation will be lost forever. But, even if they are trained they still need job opportunities.

Obama has also effectively killed millions of jobs with his attitude and attack on many industries - especially energy resources. His war on coal and oil has devastated those industries - as well as the thousands of industries that support them. One industry does not function by itself - it must have supplies, maintenance, and many other auxiliary products to function effectively. Without jobs available, where does a trained person go to find well-being and success?

Obama has destroyed their route to freedom and prosperity. Their only resort is to the streets, or to the corner waiting for a government handout. And, to be successful one must have a foundation. Historically,

America's foundation has been based on Christianity and the traditional family unit He has also attacked that foundation by casting aside Christianity and by praising non-traditional marriage.

The list of Obama's anti-Christian actions, rhetoric, and blasphemies is too long to identify each individually. A casual review of his actions and comments against churches, especially the Catholic Church, Defense of Marriage Act, cabinet appointments, and exclusion of Christian leaders from religious events are clear proof that he has no respect for God, Christian values, or any reference to the value foundation that allowed the formation of our great country - The United States of America.

# 6

# The Smoking Gun

What is Barack Obama's relationship with the Muslim Brotherhood and radical Islamists who are trying to destroy America and the Western world? Why does he refuse to call Islamic terrorists, 'terrorists?" Perhaps a statement he made in 2007 gives a fundamental clue.

On November 21, 2007, then-candidate Obama said on New Hampshire Public Radio that his Muslim experience would make us safer. He said:

"I truly believe that the day I'm inaugurated, not only the country looks at itself differently, but the world looks at America differently. If I'm reaching out to the Muslim world they understand that I've lived in a Muslim country and I may be a Christian, but I also understand their point of view.

My sister is half-Indonesian. I traveled there all the way through my college years. And so I'm intimately concerned with what happens in these countries and the cultures and perspective these folks have. And those are powerful tools for us to be able to reach out to the world. Then I think the world will have confidence that I am listening to them and that our future and our security is tied up with our ability to work with other countries in the world that will ultimately make us safer."

Is Obama delusional, or is he lost in la-la land? The radical Muslim terrorist goal is to destroy us and anyone else who is not or does not convert to Islam. Why does he think his relationship with them, or who he is, will change that dogma? But, he still refuses to criticize them and express who they really are - terrorists. Why? Does he need them for his ultimate aims? Radical includes the Muslim Brotherhood - several members are now in Obama's administration!

The 'Investigative Project on Terrorism' discovered the Islamic conspiratorial plan for the silent Islamic Jihad in America. Clearly and explicitly the proposal, and acceptance by most if not all, of these organizations is to destroy the United States and its religious foundation from WITHIN. What is Barack Obama's reaction to their plan and his attitude toward their approach? He embraces them - in his own words. This is from an interview with Steve Kroft, on 60 Minutes, where Obama made the 'bump in the road' comment after four Americans were murdered in Benghazi, and he refused to blame Islamic radicals. He said:

"Well, I've said even at the time that this is going to be a rocky path. The question presumes that somehow we could have stopped this wave of change. I think it was absolutely the right thing for us to do to align ourselves with democracy, universal rights, a notion that people have to be able to participate in their own governance.

But I was pretty certain and continue to be pretty certain that there are going to be bumps in the road because you know, in a lot of these places the one organizing principle has been Islam, the one part of society that hasn't been controlled completely by the government. There are strains of extremism, and anti-Americanism, and anti-Western sentiment. And you know can be tapped into by demagogues.

There will probably be some times where we bump up against some of these countries and have strong disagreements, but I do think that over the long term, we are more likely to get a Middle East and North Africa that is more peaceful, more prosperous and more aligned with our interests."

What did Obama say? ("the one organizing principle has been Islam, the one part of society that hasn't been controlled completely by the government.") Obama's comments fall right in line with that 'Investigative Project' report. It's the 'smoking gun' that links Obama directly to the Muslim Brotherhood intentions. He is sending them millions of our honest American dollars - while he wants more American dollars from more 'rich people.' I ask again, "What are this man's intentions?"

# 7

# Mark of the Beast

A generation ago, even just a few years ago, one could not imagine how that 'Mark of the Beast' identified in the Bible could be applied. This important reference is Revelation, Chapter 13, Verses 16 and 17, which reads:

"And he causeth all, both small and great, rich and poor, free and bond, to receive a mark in their right hand, or in their foreheads.

And, that no man might buy or sell, save he that had the mark, or the name of the beast, or the number of his name."

Those who have read my blogs also remember that the beast's name is identified by adding 6+6+6, which is 18. This can only mean 18 letters in the beast's name. Figure it out.

Anyway, suddenly it's very clear how that mark of the beast can be applied - and it's very simple and very near. Our government already has much of our personal data at the IRS. Now, the new health care system will gather even more data about us. Just yesterday, I heard that information from those two sources will be combined at a central 'Data Hub,' where the two applications can be cross-referenced for accuracy to determine eligibility and application. My new upcoming book: 'King Obama' stipulates this accumulation of personal data. My new book also explains even further. This is only one of the four conditions necessary to allow the beast's mark to be applied.

The second condition is for information gathered by the 'Prism' program to be added to the data in the government's new Data Hub. Then - the third condition - information from 'Stellar Wind,' the gigantic NSA center in Utah, will be added. Edward Snowden alerted us to these two sources that gather all information about us from our emails and phone calls and other social media - such as Facebook and Google. So, what is the fourth condition that will allow, or create, the mark of the beast?

The fourth and final condition will be when the government converts us to a 'cashless' society. If we are not allowed to use cash - you know what that means. It means everything we 'buy or sell' will be registered on a computer and that information will go straight to 'Stellar Wind' or the Data Hub. Not 'if' but 'when' that happens, anyone trying to use cash or barter likely will be considered a terror suspect. The government will know everything about us. For example, if we buy more than a usual amount of gasoline, we might get a visit from some armed person in a black suit, asking why. And, our answer better be really good!

Consider the mark in the hand or the forehead. An RFID chip with your information could be inserted in you hand between the thumb and forefinger. In the forehead? You could also memorize your 666 number if your hands are too small - or for some other physical reason. It's coming!

# 8

# Obama's Torch

Every president before Obama struggled to show America as a shining example to the rest of the world, even during times when the country struggled for mere existence and survival. Perhaps all were not totally successful, but the welfare and progress of the United States were the ideals that guided their path and their decisions. Obama's torch seems to light his path to a different direction for the future of America. His doesn't seem to be focused in the same direction as all other American presidents before him. Shouldn't the safety of citizens and the freedom to develop to their best aspirations be the highest concerns for any president or leader?

He divides the country by rhetoric and deeds, criticizing those who have been blessed by our great nation to achieve higher levels of prosperity and success. That's the success necessary to offer ladders to others to achieve even more success for themselves. Without successful people with enough to invest in opportunities for others, America would not be the shining star of the world.

Obama's actions have been to extinguish that opportunity ladder and that shining star by penalizing those who reach those success levels. He uses magnificent rhetoric to extol his virtues as an economic genius and leader who will help those at the bottom rise to middle-class, while at the same time he kicks the ladder of success from beneath them so they can remain at the bottom. His energy policies purposefully destroy jobs they could have, and increases prices on food and gas they can't afford. He kicks their opportunities out from under them - while they believe his deceptions of trying to help them.

Poor people remain at the bottom with no place to go except to the government to beg for more welfare and direct assistance. He is clearly a great deceiver. Who else has that gifted ability to smile into one's face while stabbing that same person in the back.

One of his first acts to divide Americans more was his emphasis on racism - suggesting that white people targeted black people for discrimination. He, as well as other race-baiters fail to acknowledge an important fact. White people, racists or otherwise, don't spend their time thinking about how to put down or harm black people. There's not enough time in one's life to do that, and still accomplish something for yourself or for society. Most white people spend their time and energy the same as black people - trying to do something for themselves - trying to find an avenue to make a living, and perhaps a little beyond that.

White people as well as black people have their own economic and social problems to worry about. There are more poor white people, than there are black people in total. It's been my life experience to recognize that people are people. Some black people don't like white people and some white people don't like black people. If there were any purple people, we all might dislike those purple people, equally. Regardless, the president, any president, any leader has the responsibility to bring all people together in a common cause for a country. Barack Obama has failed miserably in accomplishing this task. He hasn't even tried. In fact, he has contributed to the racial divide.

Before he can bring our races together in harmony, he must first stipulate that the problem is accentuated by both races. He doesn't have the ability or the interest to do that. Obviously, he doesn't understand the qualities necessary for 'leadership.'

# 9

# What's in a Name?

Why does Barack Obama refuse to call radical Islamic terrorists what they really are - 'Islamic Terrorists?' When forced to do so, he uses the word 'terrorism' indirectly in reference, but he never says they are 'Islamic terrorists.' Could his refusal to label them directly be based on his religious ideology connected to them? Is his long-term plan to replace our traditional American religion - Christianity - with another?

He has proclaimed that we are no longer a 'Christian' nation - not just - but only a mixture of many. He pushes the influence of Christianity out the back door as he continues to assign his Muslim brothers to higher positions of governmental authority. He quotes from the Koran to prove a point, while he mocks the Bible to discredit those who respect the Bible and worship Christ. (Remember his comments about the

24

Sermon on the Mount, "should we just stick to the Sermon on the Mount - a passage that is so radical that it's doubtful that our own Defense Department would survive its application?")

What's the purpose for his play on religious ideologies? Is it to promote himself, pretending to be a great philosopher? Is it to shape the future of the United States, which he has never specifically addressed? He has never expressed a course for our nation other than to say everyone should get their 'fair share.' Is he guiding the future of our country for himself, for the other religion, or for all citizens of our great nation? Notice how he never addresses what he hopes for future generations. He addresses only 'spreading the wealth around' now. The future would address dreams. Citizens of a country must have positive dreams. The present addresses only votes and power. Obama addresses only the present.

But why does Obama seek more power? Is that power for himself or for that other religion of a 'strange' god revealed in Daniel, Chapter 11, Verses 38 and 39? (Islam did not exist until 600 years after the death of Christ. Could a god unknown at the time of Daniel have been that 'strange' god?)

Perhaps he considers growing more worthy of occupying that high place himself without another god above him. Until that happens, however, he will need the cooperation of his Muslim brothers to help him reach that decision point.

There are two things he must have to maintain and expand his power base. He must have an active terror threat; and he must have the support of Muslims who present the facade of being cooperative and peace-loving. Now he has both.

First, he must have an ever-present danger to distract citizens that will not allow them to look toward a bright and safe future - to dream of positive things. A bright and safe future would allow American citizens to focus on more positive things such as self-improvement, country advancement, comfort, and prosperity. These are the things that define who we are - Americans. According to Maslow's 'Hierarchy of Needs' theory those higher order things cannot be approached until the safety need is fulfilled. Obama must keep the fear factor as the dominant focus so he will know exactly where the control points are - only on that one important thing to every American citizen.

Perhaps this explains why he refuses to label those groups who do harm to Americans as terrorists. He does not want to alienate them as a formal group. Perhaps he doesn't want to be seen as their adversary. To call them 'terrorists' would place a label on them that they could later use against him. But, how soon will he need them? When will their ideologies be truly and openly expressed and merged to initiate that great danger to America?

# 10

# Muslim Brotherhood

This is a little excerpt from my upcoming book, 'King Obama.' (Now published.) It expresses my concern for our future. The book contains many research entries to support all the comments.

"Why does Barack Obama and his administration

continue to court and placate the Muslim Brotherhood and known terrorist who proclaim loudly across the world, verbally and in writing that they plan to 'destroy us, our religion, and our way of life?' If they succeed, and if they fully carry out their promises, will God-fearing Americans who refuse to worship the beast (the 666 beast in the Book of Revelation) really be beheaded? It's proclaimed and it's written - why should we not believe it?

There are too many examples of Obama's support for Muslims who have expressed their plans and desires to kill Americans (Westerners and non-believers) to list in this book. All the examples on the internet would fill many volumes and many books. These examples I have presented  are only short representatives. How can anyone not believe he is an ardent Muslim terrorist supporter? He will not offend them - because he must need them for his plans for the future: The Great Imam - President for Life - King - or one identified in the Bible's Book of Revelation?

Perhaps that conclusion about Obama and his plans and actions for America must be made and accepted within each individual American heart. That thought is too dire, it's too unbelievable, to be expressed in written words in this insignificant and probably never-to-be-discovered book. But, let's look even further into Obama's acceptance of and cooperation with those who have clearly stated they intent to do harm to America.

Soon after he became President of the United States, he immediately began his silent war on Christians. Although he claims to be a Christian, that's clearly a guise to hide his real Muslim following. If he were to proclaim he is a Muslim, that would reveal the ulterior purpose for his rise to such a high worldly leadership position. Certainly, he didn't get to that position only by his own guile and actions. It took a greater force to put him there. It took a larger plan - beginning with his keynote speech during the previous Democratic National Convention. Who put him there in that position to make that speech? No one had ever heard of him. He was a great speaker, saying the right things to a large following.

He quickly revealed his large appeal plans to his 'proles' when he began his campaign for president for the 2008 election. It was "fair share" and "spread the wealth around." Of course, those voters didn't consider themselves 'proles' as identified by George Orwell. His followers were clearly thinking only of themselves and what was in it for them, personally and individually. They were blinded to the needs and the support for America's needs to support the Constitution. His supporters were diverse groups who made the election more personal - for their perceived needs, and proles' social justice.

That election was far removed from American concepts and ideologies of self-determination and self-reliance. It was guided by the concept of 'me.' Most who voted for him were blinded by his promises to do something for them - not for America. They functioned in their place in Orwell's outline of a three-tiered society perfectly."

Are we too late to recover from this attack against our Constitution and American society? Hopefully not. Hopefully, America can remain as we have envisioned it for ourselves and those who come after us.

# 11

# Samantha Power and Israel

This morning about 5:30 I was having my first cup of coffee (decaffeinated - I hate decaf, but I had several cups of regular coffee awhile back and thought I felt my heart racing, so I changed) and typing on my new Obama book and listening to news at the same time. Another of those really strange events occurred. I was typing about Samantha Power's threat and danger to Israel - and news started reporting of Power's committee hearing to replace Susan Rice as Ambassador to the United Nations.

At first, I thought I was imagining things, but it really was happening. It tweaked my interest, so I did some more research about her. I was familiar with that name because I had an article on her in my previous book, 'The Day America Died.' This is more information about the person Obama has picked to represent the United States in the United Nations. I'll probably add this information in the book I'm writing:

In a New Republic article she called for Americans to

follow the lead of German leaders post-Holocaust and apologize for their war crimes. Perhaps this was one of the reasons for Obama's 'apology tour' in 2008. She said:

"U.S. foreign policy has to be rethought. It needs not tweaking but overhauling. We need: a historical reckoning with crimes committed, sponsored, or permitted by the United States. This would entail restoring FOIA to its pre- Bush stature, opening the files, and acknowledging the force of a mantra we have spent the last decade promoting in Guatemala, South Africa, and Yugoslavia: A country has to look back before it can move forward. Instituting a doctrine of the mea culpa would enhance our credibility by showing that American decision-makers do not endorse the sins of their predecessors. When Willie Brandt went down on one knee in the Warsaw ghetto, his gesture was gratifying to World War II survivors, but it was also ennobling and cathartic for Germany."

Already one of Obama's great supporters and chief advisors she has issued statements condemning Israel. Samantha Power even recently sat on Obama's National Security Council and was a key member of the recent Benghazi event. She is extremely anti-Israel and suggests that Israel is the source of most problems in the Middle East. In an interview in 2002 she said Israel should be invaded to force them to allow Palestine to set up a separate state. She also scoffs at the idea that Iran is planning to build a nuclear bomb to use against its neighbors, especially Israel.

In a 2007 interview, Power said that America's relationship with Israel "has often led foreign policy decision-makers to defer reflexively to Israeli security assessments, and to replicate Israeli tactics..." The United States, she explained, had brought terrorist attacks upon itself by aping Israel's violations of human rights. She claimed America should be blamed for the terrorist attacks against our country.

Who is Samantha Power? She's the wife of Cass Sunstein, the recently departed Regulatory Czar in Obama's administration. He resigned, reportedly because the administration was not moving fast enough toward policies of Socialism.

# 12

# Disarming our Patriots

Restrictive activities and pressures against Americans are now being forced upon those who have sacrificed most to earn those freedoms our government is restricting - our veterans. An article by Investors.com on February 28, 2013 explains how the Obama administration is compromising veterans' rights to possess weapons. The article begins:

"Guns: Veterans who bore arms to defend their country are receiving letters that they may be declared mentally incompetent and have their Second Amendment right to keep and bear arms stripped from them. Welcome home."

The contempt by the Obama administration for our Constitution and our rights has reached a new low with news the Veterans Administration has begun sending letters to veterans telling them they will be declared mentally incompetent and stripped of the Second Amendment rights unless they can prove to unnamed bureaucrats to the contrary.

On Thursday, Michael Connelly, executive director of the United States Justice Foundation, said veterans have begun getting warning letters from the Veterans Administration (VA). The letters inform the recipients that he or she must provide evidence to the contrary within 60 days. If the veteran desires a hearing, they must inform the VA within 30 days. The letter reads:

"A determination of incompetency will prohibit you from purchasing, possessing, receiving, or transporting a firearm or ammunition. If you knowingly violate any of these prohibitions, you may be fined, imprisoned, or both pursuant to the Brady Handgun Violence Prevention Act, Pub.L.No. 103-159, as implemented at 18, United States Code 924(a)(2)."

The VA states on its Fiduciary Program website that, according to the Brady Handgun Violence Prevention Act, signed into law in 1993, being determined as unable to manage your benefits prevents you from owning and possessing a firearm or ammunition. While mental health is a factor in the current gun control debate and recent mass shootings in Newtown, Conn., and Aurora, Colo., and elsewhere have in common the questionable mental state of the shooters, to single out returning vets from Iraq and Afghanistan this way is unconscionable and unconstitutional.

No one wants the mentally unstable to possess firearms, but neither do we want to see the presumption of innocence or the right to due process guaranteed under the U.S. Constitution taken away. The Fifth Amendment states that no person shall "... be deprived of life, liberty, or property without due process of law."

The VA seems to be violating these rights to take away those guaranteed under the Second Amendment. Returning vets were seen as vulnerable to "right-wing extremists" in an April 2009 report by Janet Napolitano's Homeland Security Dept., titled "Rightwing Extremism: Current Economic and Political Climate Fueling Resurgence in Radicalization and Recruitment".

# 13

# Where is Obama?

Where is the president - the person who should be out front promoting and prompting America? Our great nation is being rocked with government scandals and irresponsibility, but our leader's voice is not heard to give courage and create confidence for citizens who want to be inspired that we are still the island that offers hope and confidence to the rest of the world. Where is Barack Obama? He takes long trips and hides on the golf course, but he's not out front encouraging Americans waiting for positive reinforcement about ourselves and our future. Perhaps he has other ideas or he would be there - out front.

Those who have occupied any type of senior

leadership position, especially in the military, understand that's the primary task of being a leader. A leader must always instill confidence and be the beacon of explaining the project ahead, whether or not it seems confusing to others. A leader should not just point in a general direction - then go hide. Where is Barack Obama?

Any leader of any country should always express and promote pride and confidence in that country. A president should be the image-maker and the promoter. Others do not have the forum - the podium - the teleprompter - to do that. It's a responsibility that should not be toyed with. Barack Obama, however, demeans America by expressing only his disdain of our country and our history. Consider the following examples expressed in his own words. These are only a few, but are representative:

April 3, 2009, in Strasbourg, France:
"There have been times when America has shown arrogance and been dismissive, even derisive."

April 6, 2009, in Ankara, Turkey:
"Another issue that confronts all democracies as they move to the future is how we deal with the past. The United States is still working through some of our own darker periods in our history."

April 17, 2009, Summit of the Americas, Trinidad and Tobago:
"While the United States has done much to promote peace and prosperity in the hemisphere, we have at times been disengaged, and at times we sought to dictate our terms."

April 20, 2009, CIA Headquarters, Langley, VA:
"Don't be discouraged that we have to acknowledge

potentially we've made some mistakes. That's how we learn."

May 21, 2009, National Archives, Washington, DC: "Unfortunately, faced with an uncertain threat, our government made a series of hasty decisions. ... I also believe that all too often our government made decisions based on fear rather than foresight; that all too often our government trimmed facts and evidence to fit ideological predispositions. Instead of strategically applying our power and our principles, too often we set those principles aside as luxuries that we could no longer afford. And during this season of fear, too many of us — Democrats and Republicans, politicians, journalists, and citizens — fell silent. In other words, we went off course."

Why isn't the president, Barack Obama, at the microphone - teleprompter - every day telling us what we need to hear - America is still the greatest country on earth, and the last best hope for mankind! Where is he?

# 14

# Is Big Brother Near?

What's moving us ever closer to that time when, according to George Orwell, we will be under the total control of "Big Brother?" We are moving ever closer than many might believe - and we are moving even faster as each day passes. We are almost there now, with four of the five components needed for that total control - almost to that point described in the Book of Revelation. What are those five components?

Requirements and conditions in the new healthcare program is the first component. That information will be centralized in a master computer and available to any part of government. It will show one's age, physical disabilities, relatives, addresses, dependency and supportive organizations - plus much other personal information. It's already combined with gun enforcement programs.

The second component is the IRS. The IRS will have much of the same information as the healthcare program - with a cross check for reliability - as well as all financial implications of every person. With only a minor twitch, the IRS could include much more information in their required personal responses.

The third components are the NSA programs that collect individual personal data. The Prism program collects data from social interaction such as Facebook, and other internet activities. That program could easily be expanded without having to get the permission or cooperation of those internet providers. What will soon tie everything together is operation 'Stellar Wind,' that giant NSA mega-computer soon to be completed in Bluffdale, Utah. Reportedly, it will have unlimited capability to collect data on every human being on earth. And, who's to say it will not be the central processor for all the other information to be combined from healthcare and the IRS? Why would one government agency want that much information? Why would we as free citizens allow it? Our basic instincts allow it. We don't protest when our government says they need it for more safety and security. According to Abraham Maslow, our basic instinct - our basic need - is safety and security.

The fourth component is the government's growing

disregard for our U.S. Constitution. Many in power claim it's outdated, and in many purposes for security, should be ignored. Or, they ignore those parts that are designed to protect our liberty and freedom without discussion or consideration by Congress. Our government, in order to gain more power and control, is using that concept to destroy our liberties. And, many among us are unconcerned enough to support that erosion of our freedom. Once lost, can we ever regain that freedom. Perhaps we should ask George Orwell and his concept of 'Big Brother.' The answer would be a resounding, "No!"

And, what is the fifth component that will tie everything together to make sure none of the pertinent information is missed? That part will be a practical answer, coming soon, and a Biblical answer. It can be found in the Book of Revelation, Chapter 13, Verses 16 and 17. I'm writing that part now in my new 'Obama' book.

# 15

# Obama Distractions

Did you ever write a book for the challenge of another purpose other than just writing a book - other than creating an interesting story with come-alive characters? In retrospect, I guess that's how I started writing novels. It wasn't just to 'write a novel.'

I wrote my first novel to see if I could create a

situation where a little girl could be the central character in a serious action-adventure theme with a touch of science fiction. I wanted it to be similar to 'Indiana Jones' but with less audacity and search for real action. That's the task I created for myself with "The Atlantis Crystal.' The mystery is 'how a little girl became attracted to crystals created when the great meteor killed the dinosaurs when it struck earth 65 million years ago - and how that was related to the demise of Atlantis. Once those characters developed themselves in that story, I had to see them through two other sequel books: 'She Waits In Atlantis' and 'Return to Atlantis.'

In my book, '666: Mark of the Beast,' I wanted to see if it would be possible to develop a story that could logically and reasonably have a battle scene similar to the last great battle in the Book of Revelation, the Apocalypse. Of course no one can interpret precisely how that last great battle unfolds, but I was very pleased how the build-up and the last scene looking across Israel's Jezreel Valley battlefield turned out. I never outline my stories, and at the end, the 'Ark of the Covenant' presented itself as a major factor, having been hinted at earlier in the book. I had no idea at that time why I even mentioned it. At this time, I haven't figured out how to write a sequel to this book. Don't think I ever will.

Perhaps my greatest satisfaction was accomplishing the goal I set for myself to write a little book, 'Shades of Retribution.' It's a post Civil War story. My goal was to write the book without a single mention of color or race, although there is about a 50-50 mix of black and white in the story. I never mentioned color even one time in the book. Those who have read it say they know who everyone is by the end of the second chapter.

I started another book a few months ago, tentatively titled, 'From Troy to Ephesus.' I got about 8,000 words, then got distracted with my 'Obama' books. When I finish the 'Obama' book I"m currently writing, I plan to make that the last one, then return to the 'Troy' book. My goal for the Troy book is to give an epic history of what happened after the Trojan War and how did the escaped Trojans later become associated with the Christian movement. (I wrote two more Obama books.)

The ruins of Ancient Troy are still in Turkey near the ruins of the seven biblical churches mentioned in the Book of Revelation. Carvings of the Trojan War were found in the ruins in Ephesus, one of those seven churches. I want to figure a way to tie them together. So far, it requires a lot of research through many cultures, and even involves the Spartan 300 and King Xerxes from Persia. Interesting. This might be my last challenging project in writing.

# 16

# No Respect

I'm just beginning Chapter 9 of my upcoming book, 'King Obama,' tentatively titled: 'Our New World.' This chapter concerns total control of all Americans, and reads:

"What permits and facilitates this movement? The components are the four parts of central government control: the healthcare law, the IRS, the new NSA center (Stellar Wind) and drones. With the combination of these four components the government can control every part of every person's life. The major component of this dangerous movement, however, is the lack of recognition or respect for our United States Constitution. Obama has demonstrated he has neither. Consider his following comments and actions that demonstrate he does not regard the Constitution as relevant."

In a 2012 interview with Matt Lauer, Barack Obama said, "Our Founding Fathers designed a system that makes it more difficult to bring about change than I would like."

What oath of office does a president take at the inauguration? Obama said, "I, do solemnly swear (or affirm) that I will faithfully execute the office of President of the United States, and I will to the best of my ability, preserve, protect, and defend the Constitution of the United States." So, is his comment that the Constitution is against the things he wishes to accomplish the same as 'defending' that Constitution? What are his other ideas and comments about the Constitution? Let's consider another that demonstrates just how dedicated he is to respecting and following the concepts designed by that Constitution.

While in the Illinois senate, in a 2001 interview, he said that the Chief Justice Earl Warren court failed to "break free from the essential constraints" in the US Constitution and launch a major redistribution of wealth. "It didn't break free from the essential constraints that were placed by the Founding Fathers in the Constitution... that generally the Constitution is a charter of negative liberties. Says what the states can't do to you. Says what the federal government can't do to you, but doesn't say what the federal government or state government must do on your behalf." Then he added the most critical comment that reveals his true purpose, "The Supreme Court never ventured into the issues of redistribution of wealth, and of more basic issues such as political and economic justice in society."

Should we consider the possibility that a president who doesn't respect our Constitution, the heart and soul of our liberty, might not totally defend that liberty?

# 17

# Is He Serious?

Is he a radical Conservative who's lost control of all logic and self-control? Asking this question of myself, of course, as I'm sure many readers of this blog often ask - or shake their heads in confusion and frustration with some of my comments. Actually, the answer is - no. I consider myself a Constitutionalist with individual opinions about certain political matters.

For example, I think it's a dangerous situation when both houses of Congress and the president are all controlled by the same party - be that Democrat or Republican. One of the three must be of the other party to keep the checks and balances as planned by our Constitution.

Did I support George W. Bush's rush to declare war on Iraq? Absolutely not! Sadam Hussein was no threat to the United States. Furthermore, Sadam Hussein's regime was the only power keeping Iran under control. They would not have allowed Iran to develop nuclear weapons! Their hatred of each other was too deep. Removing Hussein opened 'Pandora's Box.' The U.S. cannot be the police for every action throughout the world. Our first defense must be for our own citizens. Let the Islamists focus on themselves, as they have for hundreds of years, not on us. They likely will never find peace among themselves.

And, a question that many must ask is why I criticize Barack Obama so often. Actually, I don't think he directly means harm to our country. My own belief is that he is inexperienced and incompetent, and allows so much confusion that others are taking advantage. For example, on one side the Socialists are trying to slip in their charter. While, at the same time, the radical Islamists are trying to slip in the back door. In the confusion, Obama allows both to gain further advantage. In the meantime, he's only concerned about votes - for himself, and for the 2014 campaigns so he can gain both houses of Congress.

My Conservative biases appear more on the subjects of personal development, fair share, spread the wealth, and criticizing 'evil rich people.' Obama promises too much to too many people - just for their votes. Certainly, everybody should have enough to live comfortably and decently, but there should be some personal effort by individuals to achieve those conditions. My bias on this topic comes from my own family life.

My mom was born in 1921 to a sharecroppers' family. Her mother died when she was the oldest of seven siblings, at ten-years-old. She had to quit school to become the family 'mother' caregiver. She went no further than the third grade. When I was six, she started working at a shirt factory, the only industry in town. When she got off work, she then worked until dark in our cotton field, corn field, and garden. Then she spent weekends canning food and washing clothes - before running water and electricity - which we didn't have until I was twelve. She loved America, her children and her grandchildren - and she made sure I graduated high school by helping the best she could with my lessons each night. She was always there. I was the first of my extended family to graduate from high school. Her last thoughts when she left us, at eighty, was what would happen to her great-grandchildren. She was the perfect example of one who cared and one who never gave up.

Why do I criticize Obama's 'fair share' and 'spread the wealth around' comments and ideas so vehemently? He is telling people to wait and he will take care of them. That's an insult to every American - and my mom. That's denying people, who need it most, the right to work for pride and a feeling of a 'job well done.' It's also an insult to the idealisms of the American way of life. I'm not sure, but I don't think God put us here on earth to 'wait for free stuff.' Obama should encourage people to work for pride and success - not wait for it.

# 18

# Dangerous Intentions

An article reported by Clash Daily.com on March 4, 2013 reminded me of George Orwell's description of actions by the 'Thought Police.' The Thought Police are the secret police of Oceania in George Orwell's dystopian novel, '1984.' This is the article:

"Yet another student has been suspended for having something that represents a gun, but isn't actually anything like a real gun. This time, it was a breakfast pastry.

Josh Welch, a second-grader at Park Elementary School in Baltimore, Maryland, was suspended for two days because his teacher thought he shaped the strawberry, pre-baked toaster pastry into something resembling a gun. WBFF, the FOX affiliate in Baltimore, broke the story.

Welch, an arty kid who has reportedly been diagnosed with attention deficit hyperactivity disorder, said his goal was to turn it into a mountain, but that didn't really materialize, reports Fox News.

"It was already a rectangle. I just kept on biting it and biting it and tore off the top of it and kind of looked like a gun," he said. "But it wasn't," the seven-year-old astutely added.

The boy's teacher was not happy with his creation. "She was pretty mad, and I think I was in big trouble," Welch told the FOX affiliate."

This story is only one example of what's happening to innocent Americans every day. Even countless young children have been harassed and abused for things done ordinarily and naturally without a thought of hurting anyone. Just wait until it reaches the adult level - perhaps it already has?

In Orwell's book it's the job of the Thought Police to uncover and punish thoughtcrime and thought-criminals. They use psychology and omnipresent surveillance (such as telescreens) to search, find, monitor and arrest members of society who could potentially challenge authority and status quo, even only by thought, hence the name Thought Police.

I recently read Orwells's book to prepare for Chapter 8 of my new book, 'King Obama.' I haven't decided the title of the chapter yet, but it might be 'New Thought Police' or 'Political Correctness Unleashed.' The next chapter, nine, will demonstrate how the combination of the new NSA center (Stellar Wind,) IRS data, and healthcare data will be combined to give the government total view of everything we do, everything we buy, and everywhere we go. The government's new view of every citizen will eliminate the requirement for the 'Thought Police.'

# 19

# Aspirations

The new school year will be starting soon, and there are many students really desperate for help to find success in that endeavor. About 25-percent of our students nationwide suffer from lost aspirations and despair, and drop out of school. In many of the larger cities the drop-out rate is 50-percent or MORE. That usually condemns those students, those citizens, those human-beings, to sub-societal economic existence - a future of despair. When too many drop out or fail to be successful, it also strips our great nation of more positive assets we desperately need to help keep our country great.

I watched a re-run of the series 'Revolution' last night and was reminded of the great sacrifices our ancestors made to give us our freedom to make choices. One of those great choices is to become educated - as far as our aspirations will allow us to go. But those choices also require personal responsibility. Perhaps when the tug of personal responsibility is decreased, a great loss of aspirations follows. Perhaps our government's promise of a 'fair share' and free handouts has diminished that tug of responsibility, therefore the decline of personal aspirations. But, that's another story. I'm writing that book, as I take time to write this blog to offer free books to help those desperate students learn. (I'm taking my time with this new Obama political book. I want it to be all-inclusive, with fewer biblical references than my others. More people are becoming 'turned off' with the Bible, now - as prophesied in the Bible. I'm at 120 pages - about a third through.)

These two education books have been offered free several times on Amazon Kindle. They are 'Student Study Skills' and 'American Heroes: Students Who Learn.' However, I think you must be signed up with 'Prime' to download those free books. I will offer them free on Kindle again, soon, but I would prefer every child who needs these books to have them free. At the moment, the only way I know how to do that is to send a PDF copy to anyone who asks for it. If anyone has a website where it can be posted to download free, please accept the books and do that. Of course, it's copyrighted, but I authorize anyone who wants to copy them to distribute for free to please do so.

What's different about these books - than the government's efforts to 'improve education?' Government's efforts are to develop programs to get measured results - i.e. standardized testing. A child is a child, a person with feelings urged to action by certain motivations. My study skills books consider what makes a child, or anyone, decide to do something. In this case - to study. Using Maslow's 'Needs' theory, most children want to feel like they belong - usually to their peer group. Most are not driven by the basics of safety and security - or the higher levels of esteem and self-actualization. They want to feel they are comfortable in a group they understand. All government's education programs totally ignore this concept. A child wants to be in an accepted group - but most want a little esteem; to be on the upper edge of that group. They don't want to be labeled a 'bookworm' as many of us were when we were children - but they want that extra recognition.

# 20

# Things Just Happen

How does someone become involved with events and circumstances alien to their plans or intentions? Sometimes it seems 'things just happen that way.'

When I retired from the Air Force in 1978, I already had my real estate broker's license and opened a real estate office in Tracy, CA, which was the location of my last assignment at the defense depot located there. I had also taught real estate college courses while I was stationed overseas. Housing was booming in California at that time, and I just assumed everything would work out okay - I would make a lot of money - be a real estate 'tycoon' - and retire early. Things were going well, and a year later I opened another office in Stockton. My, how things can change so suddenly. Jimmy Carter became president: longer lines were forming at gas stations - and home mortgage rates went from 9-percent to 16-percent overnight. Suddenly my plans to be a real estate 'tycoon' ended when people couldn't qualify for home loans.

After six months of all expenses and no income, I decided I really didn't want to be a real estate tycoon anyway. I decided I should be a working man, 'a man of sweat and toil,' so I joined a major security system company and became their distribution manager. That was the time of great 'downsizing' so I was moved from

Hayward, CA to Jonesboro, AR, to Memphis, TN, as the central distribution center manager. I wrote my first book while I was in Jonesboro. It was titled, 'Simply Success' and was based on my observations and correlations between managing military people and civilians. There was a standard process to success that I had observed in both environments.

I lived in Southaven, MS when I worked in Memphis. I was also focusing on writing more management-leadership-success books. I think I self-published two at that time - and you know what happens when you have a stack of books in your garage. I quit my job to focus on writing, and to begin volunteer work for the local Chamber of Commerce. I became their publicity director and did all their photo-publicity work.

John Grisham was a lawyer in Southaven at that time and was trying to get discovered with his legal thrillers. Scott Turow had opened the doors for that genre and John happened along at the right time. He was also a state representative, which gave him lots of exposure as he traveled around selling books from his automobile. His first book was 'A Time To Kill' although his first agent published book was 'The Firm.' John quickly moved to Oxford to claim that residency, because for personal reasons he did not want Southaven to claim him as their popular successful author.

With John's success in fiction, I changed my emphasis to fiction and wrote my first novel which was 'The Atlantis Crystal.' Before that, I wrote a little practice novel, 'School Bells and Broken Tales: Exploring With Jack and Jill,' that had a slightly educational venue that got me invited into school programs. I was also the president of the local Optimist Club for five years, which gave me even more exposure to the education environment. Before I knew what happened, I was considered an 'education' person by the local community. That led to my creation of a program called

'SaYes' which is an acronym for 'Study Attitudes Yield Education Success.' Eventually, I got the state governor's senior education advisor and the local schools involved to prove that education results could be improved. And we did prove that it could be done.

Shortly afterward, the federal government took over most of the school programs and requirements - and you know what happened after that. That's why I have expressed many times that the U.S. Department of Education should not only be eliminated - it should be wiped off the face of the earth. They focus on their goals - not on the goals and needs of individual students.

This is getting a little long, so I will stop here for now. My next blog, hopefully tomorrow (I'm still pretty occupied writing that other political book) I will give some more information about using the concept of Abraham Maslow's 'Hierarchy of Needs' theory to create effective education. Also, since school will be starting soon, I will also offer a free study skills book for any parent or grandparent who wants one for their child or grandchild - or any other student. You can preview them here or on Amazon. They are 'Student Study Skills' and 'American Heroes: Students Who Learn.'

# 21

# A Good Man?

I've been somewhat criticized recently by two of my AD friends about my over-zealous criticism of Barack Obama, especially pertaining to my interpretation of his actions regarding Muslims, socialism, etc. I also learned that my observations were 'nonsense.' I was also informed that Obama is a 'good man' and a 'true American.' So, taking those comments to heart, I will present a blog about Obama without those criticisms and 'nonsense.' In this blog, I will only ask questions.

1. If Obama is a 'good man' why did he cast aside and abandon his long-time 'good friend' and mentor, Jeremiah Wright, when Wright became a burden to him?

2. If he is a 'true American' why did he not criticize the Black Panther members who intimidated white voters at a voting place in Philadelphia during the 2008 campaign? Why did he allow Eric Holder to dismiss that case?

3. If Obama is a 'true American' why did he label a young white police officer a racist for questioning a black man who appeared to be breaking into a house - although it was his house? Wouldn't a 'good man' have

asked for the facts before condemning someone - and calling him a racist?

4. Why did Barack Obama refuse to allow Eric Holder to give Congress information about operation 'Fast and Furious?' Operation Fast and Furious resulted in the loss of over 2000 weapons, the deaths of hundreds of Mexicans, and the death of a Border Patrol agent. Doesn't Congress and citizens have a right to know why one of our own was murdered? What happened to most of the 2000 weapons? Why did his administration order 1.6 billion rounds of ammunition for similar weapons?

5. During the 2012 campaign, although Obama didn't personally criticize the TEA party, his staff were totally vitriolic against them. As a result, obviously to support Obama, did the IRS intimidate TEA party groups who submitted for tax-exempt status? If Obama wasn't involved, why did the IRS head visit the White House at least 51 times that year?

6. Why did Barack Obama not censure, reprimand, or ask for Eric Holder's resignation when Holder falsely accused a news reporter of being a participant in a criminal activity? Does that sound like a good man or a true American?

7. To me, the Benghazi event raises the most serious questions for a Commander-in-Chief. Where was Barack Obama during the Benghazi activity? He has never said. Where was Hillary Clinton during the massacre of four brave Americans fighting for their lives? She has never said. Military units were on stand-by to intervene - to try to offer aid to those four people who knew they were going to die if they didn't get help. Stand-by units were told to stand down. Who gave that order? Where was

Barack Obama? He refuses to say where he was or what he was doing. Is that the response of a 'true American?' Is that not the responsibility of a real Commander-in-Chief?

8. What's Obama's real purpose for the secret program "Stellar Wind" being built in Bluffdale, Utah? It can review phone calls and emails of every person on earth. What are his plans for it?

9. How does Barack Obama keep his hands clean from all the negative activity and scandals in his administration? Why doesn't he say where he is when all these things are happening? Is he perpetrating these activities - then hiding from scrutiny?

10. Finally, why does every discussion of Barack Obama's weaknesses always involve a comparison with George W. Bush? Should Obama be compared to other presidents, forever, or should he be evaluated on fulfilling his own responsibilities as the current president of the United States? George Bush is not the president - and he is prohibited by the Constitution from ever being president again!

# 22

# A New Low

A report by Investors.com, a part of Investors Business Daily, on June 26, 2013, disclosed the following information:

"In a new low for an administration that courts U.S. enemies, the White House has met secretly with the deputy of a Muslim cleric who has called for the killing of U.S. troops. On June 13, the National Security Council hosted Sheik Abdullah bin Bayyah for a West Wing chat, where the radical Islamist asked for more support for Hamas and Syrian 'rebels,' i.e. al-Qaida terrorists."

Information such as this prompted me to write another book. It's tentatively titled: 'King Obama,' but I could change it to 'President-For-Life' or 'The Great Imam.' Anyway, at the moment, the following is the back matter for the book. I should have it finished sometimes this month:

"Why does Barack Obama and his administration continue to court and placate the Muslim Brotherhood and known terrorists who proclaim loudly across the world, verbally and in writing, that they plan to destroy us, our religion, and our way of life? If they succeed, and if they fully carry out their promises, will God-fearing Americans who refuse to worship the beast, as predicted in the Bible, really be beheaded? It's proclaimed and it's written - why should we not believe it?

There are too many examples of Obama's support for Muslims who have expressed their plans and desires to kill Americans (Westerners and non-believers) to list in this book. All the examples on the internet would fill many volumes and many books. These examples are only short representatives. How can anyone not believe he is an ardent Muslim terrorist supporter? He will not offend them and he will not call them 'terrorists' - because perhaps he needs them for plans for his future: The Great Imam - President for Life - King - or one identified in the Bible's Book of Revelation?"

This might be the last book I'm allowed to write criticizing Obama and my view of his destiny for our future. Hopefully, my interpretations have been totally in error. Hopefully, these thoughts have been only delusions of one with a totally lost view of reality. I believe our great country has the basis and the foundation - and the good people - to last far into the future. Whatever happens to me, nevertheless, it's been a great ride in a to-now great country.

# 23

# Two Terms

My observations and reporting of Islamic concerns have been somewhat in question, recently, so I thought I should give a brief comment on the basis of my concerns. Fundamentally, the Muslim doctrine is for every person on earth to be a Muslim, even if they must be forced. If not, they are to be killed. The world must become 'pure.' That's 'pure' Muslim. That's their WRITTEN charter. Should we believe them or should we ignore them as a joke. I believe they mean what they say! It's also a strong indicator that the antichrist, the beast, will be a Muslim. The one who will make the world pure, according to Islam, is their Mahdi.

The Investigative Report on Terrorism located a document in 1991 that revealed the plan of Muslims to take over the United States with a 'Silent or Civilization Jihad.' Basically, that document revealed that all Muslim organizations in the United States would work toward that aim, and would be under the general guidance of the Islamic Society of North America (ISNA.) That organization is even larger today, with much more influence, and many of its members are an integral and official part of the Obama administration - some even still openly expressing their support for major terrorist groups.

Revelation, Chapter 20,Verse 4 says the souls of those who are beheaded by the beast because they had not worshiped him or his image, or had not received his mark upon their foreheads or in their hands would live and reign with Christ a thousand years. Daniel, Chapter 11, Verses 38 and 39 state, "But in his estate shall he honour the God of forces; and a god whom his fathers knew not shall he honour with gold, and silver, and with precious stones, and pleasant things. This shall he do in the most strong holds with a strange god, whom he shall acknowledge and increase with glory; and he shall cause them to rule over many, and shall divide the land for gain."

Two points in these references suggest the 'beast' will be a Muslim. First, the only groups who like to behead people are Muslims. Daniel references a 'strange god.' When Daniel wrote this comment, Muslims or their god did not exist. That happened six hundred years after Christianity. Daniel didn't know what to call that god - except strange. Although Obama claims to be a Christian - he gives more of his time and support to Muslims. What will happen in the future, when Muslims have more influence in the United States? Do they see Obama as their Mahdi?

I also heard Obama's speech this morning in South Africa. He praised Nelson Mandela and George Washington for serving only two terms as president - saying that was an honorable thing. If he really believes that, then why is he now promoting his 'Organizing for Action' group in all 50 states? Why did he even mention 'two terms?' Likely, he well understands the Muslim practice of 'taqiyya' to advance his future plans. I'm about half finished writing a new book, 'King Obama.'

# 24

# Traitors

Barack Obama and his minions are now trying to track down and capture the "traitor" Edward Snowden for leaking America's secrets to our enemies, particularly China and Russia. This important chase causes me to ask two questions. First, what information did Snowden reveal that has not been already known publicly. Second, who is (are) the real American traitors?

Those actions by the NSA were announced way before Snowden's revelations. My blog on May 25th, titled: The Looming Big Brother, reported a story by Wired Magazine that gave essentially the same information. It said the whole world was 'being hacked.' This is the important paragraph from that blog:

"A new story in Wired Magazine reveals details about how the National Security Agency is quietly building the largest spy center in the country in Bluffdale, Utah, as part of a secret   surveillance program codenamed "Stellar Wind." According to investigative reporter James Bamford, the NSA has established listening posts throughout the nation to collect and sift through billions of email messages and phone calls, whether they originate within the country or overseas."

Who are America's real traitors - if that's the word the Obama administration chooses to use? Could we consider Joe Biden and Barack Obama? They have done more damage to American citizens than Edward Snowden could ever do.

On May 1, 2011, Barack Obama personally and proudly gave the announcement on the killing of Osama Bin Laden. That briefing contained 'classified' information. Then on May 3, only three days later at a Washington event, Joe Biden announced the raid was carried out by SEAL Team 6. That was even more dangerous 'classified' information. Within hours, a member of SEAL Team 6 called his mother and told her to "wipe every piece of information regarding the family on social media, Facebook and Twitter." According to the mother, he said, "Mom, we're picking up chatter. We're not safe. You're not safe. Delete everything."

On Aug. 6, 2011, a Chinook helicopter carrying 30 U.S. service members — including 15 SEAL Team 6 members — was shot down in Afghanistan. Everyone on board was killed. The Chinook was shot down by a Taliban rocket-propelled grenade in Wardak province. Taliban fighters were waiting on three sides for the aircraft as it approached. The Chinook was a sitting duck as it hovered in the sky.

The evidence is overwhelming and disturbing: SEAL Team 6 members were ambushed. It was America's single greatest loss of life in Afghanistan and the largest number of SEALs ever killed in one incident in history. The strange part is that some of the Afghan soldiers on the helicopter were replaced just before the helicopter took off.

And, to show his true 'patriotism' Barack Obama has appointed five Islamists as czars and senior advisors to his administration. They are all connected with the

Islamic Society of North America (ISNA) whose WRITTEN GOAL is to make America a Sharia nation. They are: Imam Mohamed Magid, Salam al-Marayati, Rashid Hussain, Mohammed Elibiary, and Arif Alikhan. Several are appointed to Homeland Security.

So, of these three people, who has done the most damage to American citizens? Who has the greatest potential to destroy the America we know and love?

# 25

# Proud Americans

I just got back from one of my best trips ever - in San Antonio, TX. It was the 50$^{th}$ anniversary reunion of my Air Force Officer Candidate School (OCS) class. We graduated June 21$^{st}$, 1963, at Lackland Air Force Base in San Antonio, Texas. The OCS program began in Miami Beach, FL. Our class was the last Air Force OCS class, and closed the doors on the long institution that began in 1942. Then it was the Army Air Corp. The Air Force became a separate service in 1947. Many in that first class in 1942 went on to become famous movie stars.

Clark Gable was a graduate of class 42E, and went on to become an Army Major. Some of the many other graduates who later had famous careers were: Gilbert Roland, Bill Holden, Robert Preston and Ben Hogan. None of my classmates ever achieved even close to that level of fame, nevertheless, we were all equally proud graduates of that institution. One classmate became a one-star general and one became a two-star general. Most retired with the rank of between major and colonel. I didn't stay in long enough to make colonel, and retired as a major at 21years service.

We were all selected from the enlisted ranks as a member of the Air Force, based on a qualification test and service record. Those who entered the program began the six-month program as an E-3 to an E-6. At the time I entered, I was an E-4 and had been in the Air Force six years. I was 24 years old, and the age limit was 26. It was a career path where one could become an Air Force officer without having a college degree first. Of course to get promoted we had to rapidly get our degree.

My graduating class had 120 members. Now, there are only 90 of us left. Most of those who departed were by natural causes. One was a pilot shot down over North Vietnam and became a MIA. He was never recovered and was later declared dead. Those of us remaining are between the ages of 72 to 76. Our next reunion is scheduled for two years from now. I wonder ----. Anyway, that program changed the lives of 120 proud Americans - who became even more eager to demonstrate pride in America and the great opportunities our forefathers gave us. Perhaps this might help explain why I am so adamant to help preserve that institution that I believe some in our government are trying to destroy.

# 26

# Watching

While I was having my first cup of coffee this morning and watching Fox News to catch up on overnight events  my mind wandered off a little into 'What If' land. Then one of the TV hosts said, "And, if you have an ADT security camera in your home, the government can even be watching everything you do." This was referencing the NSA security question. Since I was an ADT distribution manager for several years, that caught my attention and sent my thoughts into overdrive. It reminded me of Winston in George Orwells' book about Big Brother. Winston was the main character, trying to find peace within the system. The telescreen was always watching him. He finally found a hideaway to make love with a woman, but that was also a trap.

Written in 1949, Orwell's idea of an all-intrusive telescreen was somewhat futuristic, but it's an idea that exploded beyond imagination. Now, that telescreen that could be seen and somewhat avoided at that time has taken on a different character. Now that 'telescreen' can be the size of a pinhead, placed anywhere, and transmitting a wireless signal. As a fiction writer, can you imagine the implications of that?  In the name of 'safety and security' our not-too-transparent government is moving further away from individual liberty and freedom. The scrutiny gets tighter.

What are these implications for a fiction writer? Suppose your writing sees a few years into the future, such as a scene I used a few years ago with a cell phone thrown on a garbage truck to escape pursuers. The bad guys tracked the cell phone to the garbage dump, instead of following the good guys. Now, that wouldn't be an unusual scenario.

Now, the bad guys can watch you from the sky and fire a bullet from a drone right through your heart. But, suppose in your writing, you included an imagined event known only to the secret intelligence world as reality. What might happen to you? Where would the telescreen be watching you; how many telescreens; and could they see you in the dark? Could Big Brother analyze the document section of your computer? If you tried to write a novel by hand, instead of typing on the computer, would that be considered a dangerous activity by a Big Brother government?

These are similar questions Winston faced. He didn't know who was watching, where they were watching or how often they were watching. Although Winston never did anything wrong he didn't escape. He didn't even know what he didn't escape from. Big Brother needed too much security.

# 27

# Well - Excuse Me

I keep trying to work on my new novel, 'From Troy to Ephesus,' but I keep getting distracted with more revelations about Obama's intentions for our great country. I just recalled that not a single cabinet member, advisor, or supporter of Obama has ever had anything positive to say about America. Then I remembered something about Samantha Power that I had reviewed before. She is Obama's new choice to be the Ambassador to the United Nations, replacing Susan Rice. I'll report on anti-American stances of Susan Rice and John Kerry later. But now for Samantha Power:

Philip Klein of the Washington Examiner reported that in a 2003 op-ed attacking the Bush administration in the liberal 'New Republic,' Samantha Power proposed a "doctrine of the mea culpa" that would supposedly raise America's stature in the eyes of the world, likening it to the historic example of German Chancellor Willy Brandt kneeling at a Warsaw ghetto memorial. She wrote:

"We need a historical reckoning with crimes committed, sponsored, or permitted by the United States. This would entail restoring FOIA to its pre-Bush stature, opening the files, and acknowledging the force of a mantra we have spent the last decade promoting in Guatemala, South Africa, and Yugoslavia. A country has to look back before it can move forward. Instituting a doctrine of the mea culpa would enhance our credibility by showing that American decision-makers do not endorse the sins of their predecessors. When Willie Brandt went down on one knee in the Warsaw ghetto, his gesture was gratifying to World War II survivors, but it was also ennobling and cathartic for Germany. Would such an approach be futile for the United States?"

Klein's report continues, "Contrary to Democrat accusations that Romney made up the apology tour scenario out of thin air, Power is on record pushing for U.S. foreign policy to be completely re-worked so as to tell the world we are sorry. Power even implied that the kinds of horrors Nazis committed toward Jews have been carried out by the U.S. against other people around the world. In that context, Obama's visit to Allied-bombed Dresden, on a tour that included the Buchenwald concentration camp, may seem to make sense after all."

Clearly, Samantha Power is a real danger to the security of the United States by any exercise of power or influence in or near the White House. Since she was also involved in the Benghazi event, clearly her promotion to a higher level and more visible position is her reward for being a 'good soldier' for Obama's plans for America. His plans, certainly most devious, cannot be for the betterment of freedom and democracy. If that's not the case, then why is he keeping so many secrets? Why is everyone in his administration refusing to tell the truth, or anything, about their activities? They are hiding everything. Why? Does Samantha Power need to be representing the United States in a United Nations forum?

# 28

# In Awe

I had one of the greatest experiences of my life this morning. Of course, just living life with a lovely family and with many good friends is a fantastic journey, but this was very different on an even more personal level. If you read my blog posts you know most are very serious. That's because I'm a retired military officer who still respects the oath to defend my country against all enemies - foreign and domestic. Now, I feel the most serious threats to our freedom is from within. However, ordinarily in my day-to-day life I have a much softer side. I can find happiness in just exploring the feeling of taking in a full breath of air. I am aware God put the air there for me to breath.

For some reason, this morning was special. I did my usual: got up at five, had my cereal, put a cup of water in the microwave to make coffee, then went outside to get the paper so it would be on the table for my wife when she got up.

Before I leaned over to pick up the paper, I stopped in total awe. There were at least five different types of birds chirping and singing all around me - the world was totally alive with majestic sounds. Instinctively, I looked up and said, "Thank you, God." (Even sitting inside, now, at my computer, I still hear the mocking birds loud mouths chirping.)

Before I picked up the paper, I listened to all the individual songs and tried to imagine - Why? Then my inner voice answered that it was to help start the day with beauty - to begin on the positive side with a feeling that all life is precious. Then I tried to imagine what it would be like if there were no precious sounds to begin the day. There would be only a weird silence of our globe whirling through space - if that makes a sound. The other would be the sound of blood swishing its way through our arteries and veins. Can you imagine the distraction of only  hearing blood pulsate past your ear sensors?

Then, I imagined further and considered that every space of our earth is filled with life: germs filling the air; and worms, mold, germs, and many other large and small creatures occupying the dirt. The last thing I murmured to myself before I picked up the paper was, "Can you imagine anyone not believing God exists - and His existence is to make life wonderful for his followers here on earth."

# 29

# Deceptions

Many who read my blogs that are usually highly-charged against Barack Obama's leadership and actions might wonder if I've lost my mind - if I'm off my rocker. I often wonder that, even myself, until another event pops up that slams the same questions in my face: Is he telling the truth? Is that in the best interest of America?

If there weren't so many of his followers who worship him as their God, I wouldn't spend so much of my time researching and writing about his deviations and the danger I feel he presents to our country. But, with nearly half our population instinctively believing that their Obama God can do no wrong, there must be someone who questions that religious devoutness. There must be some balance to reason.

He can remain in control of our wonderful country, forever, with only a gentle support from an undecided few. Hillary Clinton and Joe Biden are looking forward to their opportunity for 2016. There's a strong possibility they will never get that chance. Obama's worshipers will demand his presence. And, don't be fooled - there are ways he can do it. Who could stop him? Our Constitution has no definition of how to stop one who would assume total power - even if the Supreme Court condemns it. Our military is not allowed to act!

Obama's whole time in office has been one long deception, beginning with his birth certificate. Why did it take him over a year to finally present one that he claims is his. Why did he send a special courier to Hawaii to retrieve it? He doesn't allow information to be presented to Congress about 'Operation Fast and Furious.' What happened to 2500 high-powered weapons.

Then there's the Benghazi question: who ordered the military stand down? Obama is stifling that information - only the president has the authority to do that. What was he doing while four patriots were being slaughtered valiantly serving their country?

Does anyone really believe he was not involved with the IRS targeting of his opponents? Why did his IRS chief visit his office 157 times during that activity? These are enough examples - there are too many to list during the next eight hours.

With all my posts about Obama, some might wonder if I'm concerned about my welfare and safety. I'm human - of course I'm concerned, but not to the point of being paralyzed by fear. At 74, I've lived almost one-third the life of our great nation. It's been a wonderful life of ups and downs, fear and delight, and wins and losses. With that experience, the thing I see now for our country is danger that it's never faced before. A younger person ordinarily doesn't have the freedom to express some things, even if he or she understands. The family and making a living must take priority. The worst Obama can do to me is make me disappear. Could he also make FOX news disappear? Interesting.

# 30

# No More Secrets

Recently, I posted a blog reporting information about the new NSA spy center being built in Utah. That blog includes this quote:

"A new story in Wired Magazine reveals details about how the National Security Agency is quietly building the largest spy center in the country in Bluffdale, Utah, as part of a secret surveillance program codenamed "Stellar Wind." According to investigative reporter James Bamford, the NSA has established listening posts throughout the nation to collect and sift through billions of email messages and phone calls, whether they originate within the country or overseas.

The Utah spy center will contain near-bottomless databases to store all forms of communication collected by the agency. This includes the complete contents of private emails, cell phone calls and Google searches, as well as all sorts of personal data trails including: parking receipts, travel itineraries, bookstore purchases and other digital "pocket litter."

According to this report, this center will have almost endless ability to collect data. Built under the Obama administration, this is a highly dangerous endeavor that will curtail our liberty and freedom - in the name of safety and security. This concept is based on Maslow's 'Hierarch of Needs' motivation theory: survival, safety, belonging, esteem, self-actualization. Accordingly, the safety need must be fulfilled before the higher-order needs can affect one's motivations. 'Stellar Wind' is to focus our thoughts only on safety and security, disregarding liberty and freedom. In observing Obama's actions and words - he knows exactly what he's doing to destroy our once great nation. What could be planned?

When IRS data and health care data are merged into this system, the government will know - INSTANTLY - when you sneeze or buy a roll of toilet paper. For women, they will know the ovulation period by their purchases. They will know who is incontinent and who is buying birth control items.

Although at the moment they haven't banned firearms, they will know the instant you buy a hunting rifle, shotgun, or pistol - including air rifles; and they will know the serial numbers and the amount of ammunition: instantly! The next step will be universal firearm registration, so there will be no secret threats to the pending total government autocratic takeover.

Then, what's the next step? A cashless society - so every transaction must be recorded. And, what's the next step? Read Revelation, Chapter 13, Verses 16-18.

In effect, this NSA center will have the capability to support any 'Big Brother' activities the Obama administration would wish to initiate. His supporters have already begun to set the stage for Obama's next move. How much stronger will he make his IRS enforcers - especially after they begin controlling Obamacare?

With that information and control over every American citizen, in the most minute detail, how soon will it be before you will get a phone call from 'Big Brother' asking why you bought 'too much' outdoor life survival equipment - or more than your fair share of 'edible plants' for your garden? I wish this were a joke, but it's not! Our government - Barack Obama - will have enough information about you to ask those questions. They probably already have that information

# 31

## Ingenuity

Very strange —. I just saw a news report that some terrorists were foiled in their plot to spread nerve gas and mustard gas in the United States and Europe. That was only two minutes ago as I type this message. At the same time, I was thinking of how to incorporate my fictional account of how terrorists moved canisters of gas across our southern borders to use in attacks against Americans. That fictional account is in my novel, 'America 20XX: The New World Order.'

In my new writing (fictional) I'm going to show how a leader who wants to be 'President for life' could allow or create a terrorist incident that would allow him to reasonably declare 'martial law' and eliminate voting until the crisis was over. Of course, in reality, we know that could never happen in America - or could it?

In this current news report, the really strange coincidence is that the mode of delivery is eerily similar. In my book, the gas canisters were dropped by parachute from ultra-lite aircraft onto the desert in a designated area seen only in a black light mode from above. Those gas canisters were to be used by terrorists waiting on the ground with their black light detectors. The news report I just heard said that in the foiled attempt, terrorists planned to release gas from toy airplanes. The purpose for the story in my book is to demonstrate that there is no limit to the possibilities terrorists will use to attack us.

Another example in my book, is that toy remote controlled boats can also be used in devious and cunning terrorists activities. This example in the book demonstrates how a toy boat could deliver a leader-line to the opposite side of the Rio Grande near El Paso to transfer weapons underwater during the dead of night. Does this seem far-fetched? Look into the mind of a dedicated and desperate terrorist and realize that nothing is impossible or inconceivable. That reality is the purpose for that book.

# 32

# Important Issues

This is part of a 'letter to the editor' that appeared in my local newspaper on May 27, 2013. Below that extract is my response that I will submit to the newspaper, after June 1st:

"Now that President Obama is in his second term,

legislators are again trying to undermine his objectives for the country. At every opportunity -- Benghazi and the IRS, for examples -- legislators direct our focus away from the important issues confronting us. Legislators attempt to turn back time to the days when women had no rights to their own health and welfare. To the days before unions and the middle-class they helped to create. To those times when the elderly had no Social Security or Medicare to cushion them from life's hardships --- To the "Wild West," in which everyone could tote a gun anywhere."

This is my pending response to that letter:

"In Mary Larson's letter, May 27, 2013: 'Playing politics does not get the job done,' she criticized legislators for not supporting Obama's social agenda. 'At every opportunity -- Benghazi and the IRS, for examples -- legislators direct our focus away from the important issues confronting us.' Perhaps she is unaware that government actions are guided by our Constitution - not by important issues. The first goal of our Constitution is individual liberty. The first order of the commander-in-chief is to protect citizens from harm.

During the Benghazi massacre, should Barack Obama have been focused on how to get more free birth control pills to more women (for their health care) or should he have been trying to rescue four brave Americans fighting for their lives? Regarding the IRS, should he have been guiding fair and equitable treatment to all citizens - or prompting more oppression against his political opponents, as was the case in his speeches? Regarding the press, why did he make derogatory comments about FOX News, which emboldened Eric Holder to charge a reporter, falsely, with a crime against America? Are these Constitutional issues not important issues?

She also mocked the right to own personal weapons as the "Wild West." Is she unaware that jihadists from Iran and Yemen are now training in Brazil, Argentina, and Paraguay to attack Americans if Iran is threatened by us or by Israel? How comfortable would she feel living unarmed on our southern border? Would words about "important issues," save her life, if attacked by those terrorists?"

Her letter reminded me of a concept that I just read in George Orwell's book, '1984,' (The Big Brother book.) Under a section he titled: IGNORANCE IS STRENGTH, he identified three kinds of people: the High, Middle, and Low. The aim of the High is to remain where they are, the aim of the Middle is to get to the High, and the aim of the Low is to abolish all distinctions and create a society where all men will be equal. According to Orwell, the Middle uses the Low to achieve their goals by pretending they are fighting for "liberty and justice." Once their goals are fulfilled they ignore the Low and cast them back to where they were. Of the three groups, only the Low are never even temporarily successful in achieving their aims. They continue to be used by the Middle to achieve their aims.

Is it possible Obama read this book then created his 'fair share' mantra? Is his original power base now beginning to realize they have been used - for him to achieve his aims? Maybe now union members can offer that answer.

# 33

# Gestapo Actions

How does a country fail? What allows tyranny to prevail? Consider this comment in a local 'Letter to the Editor' that appeared today:

"Now that President Obama is in his second term, legislators are again trying to undermine his objectives for the country. At every opportunity -- Benghazi and the IRS, for examples -- legislators direct our focus away from the important issues confronting us."

Too many of our citizens have this same attitude about Obama. They believe his government bullying is make believe, and these Gestapo actions by our government are unimportant. Should we ignore these early warning signs of government tyranny and social, cultural, and moral decline? Consider this story from Investors Business Daily:

"The inexplicable raid nearly two years ago on a guitar maker for using allegedly illegal wood that its competitors also used was another targeting by this administration of its political enemies. On Aug. 24, 2011, federal agents executed four search warrants on Gibson Guitar Corp. facilities in Nashville and Memphis,

Tenn., and seized several pallets of wood, electronic files and guitars. One of the top makers of acoustic and electric guitars, including the iconic Les Paul introduced in 1952, Gibson was accused of using wood illegally obtained in violation of the century-old Lacey Act, which outlaws trafficking in flora and fauna the harvesting of which had broken foreign laws.

In one raid, the feds hauled away ebony fingerboards, alleging they violated Madagascar law. (Not U.S. law) Gibson responded by obtaining the sworn word of the African island's government that no law had been broken. In another raid, the feds found materials imported from India, claiming they too moved across the globe in violation of Indian law. (Not U.S. law) Gibson's response was that the feds had simply misinterpreted Indian law.

Interestingly, one of Gibson's leading competitors is C.F. Martin & amp; Co. According to C.F. Martin's catalog, several of their guitars contain "East Indian Rosewood," which is the exact same wood in at least 10 of Gibson's guitars. So why were they not also raided and their inventory of foreign wood seized? (Over 95 percent of this wood goes to China to make expensive $800,000 beds.)

Grossly under-reported at the time was the fact that Gibson's chief executive, Henry Juszkiewicz, contributed to Republican politicians. Recent donations have included $2,000 to Rep. Marsha Blackburn, R-Tenn., and $1,500 to Sen. Lamar Alexander, R-Tenn. By contrast, Chris Martin IV, the Martin & amp; Co. CEO, is a long-time Democratic supporter, with $35,400 in contributions to Democratic candidates and the Democratic National Committee over the past couple of election cycles.

Gibson described "two hostile raids on its factories by agents (over 30 agents as reported later) carrying weapons and attired in SWAT gear where employees were forced out of the premises, production was shut down, goods were seized as contraband and threats were made that would have forced the business to close." Gibson, fearing a bankrupting legal battle, settled and agreed to pay a $300,000 penalty to the U.S. Government. It also agreed to make a "community service payment" of $50,000 to the National Fish and Wildlife Foundation to be used on research projects or tree-conservation activities. The feds in return agreed to let Gibson resume importing wood while they sought "clarification" from India.

The Gibson Guitar raid, the IRS intimidation of Tea Party groups and the fraudulently obtained warrant naming Fox News reporter James Rosen as an "aider, abettor, co-conspirator" in stealing government secrets are but a few examples of the abuse of power by the Obama administration to intimidate those on its enemies list."

Should half our population continue to ignore these clear signs of growing government tyranny and support this Obama administration - as began the rise of other dangerous autocratic governments? Should Obama zealots continue to support the Obama mission - to harass and intimidate anyone who disagrees with his plans for our country? Again, I repeat: Obama will not give up the presidency at the end of his current term.

# 34

# Military Actions

I just finished reading the book, '1984' by George Orwell. It's the book that initiated the concept of 'Big Brother.' A major part of the story includes the use of 'telescreens' and hidden microphones to watch and listen to every citizen in almost every environment. It also incorporates the use of 'Thought Police' who monitor facial expressions to determine citizens' probable thoughts and intentions. A wrong facial expression or out-of-place thought causes a citizen to disappear for awhile or be instantly 'vaporized.' This idea reminded me of the new NSA center being built in Utah. I copied the information, below, about that center:

"A new story in Wired Magazine reveals details about how the National Security Agency is quietly building the largest spy center in the country in Bluffdale, Utah, as part of a secret  surveillance program codenamed "Stellar Wind." According to investigative reporter James Bamford, the NSA has established listening posts throughout the nation to collect and sift through billions of email messages and phone calls, whether they originate within the country or overseas.

The Utah spy center will contain near-bottomless databases to store all forms of communication collected by the agency. This includes the complete contents of private emails, cell phone calls and Google searches, as well as all sorts of personal data trails including: parking receipts, travel itineraries, bookstore purchases and other digital "pocket litter."

In effect - this center will have the capability to support any 'Big Brother' activities the Obama administration would wish to initiate. His supporters have already begun to set the stage for Obama's next move. How much stronger will he make his IRS enforcers? How much more pressure will be put on media researchers and reporters to deny them the right to inform the public? How much more pressure and intimidation will he use to prevent those within his administration from revealing devious plans? How much more support will he continue to give his radical Muslim supporters? When his 'Thought Police' have the addresses of every gun sold in America, how soon will his purge begin?

Of course there are many more important questions regarding this impending danger. Probably the most important is: will our American military fire on any citizen who refuses to give up his or her firearm? Will they have a choice? They should begin asking themselves that question, now, before they have to make that decision.

# 35

# Obama's Bait

I'm still reading George Orwell's book, '1984' concerning 'Big Brother,' and finally reached an interesting comment on page 166. Thank goodness it wasn't page '666.' That would have been even more profound. Anyway, this comment classifies society as the High, Middle, and Low. Orwell writes:

"The aim of the Low, when they have an aim - for it is an abiding characteristic of the Low that they are too much crushed by drudgery to be more than intermittently conscious of anything outside their daily lives - is to abolish all distinctions and create a society in which all men shall be equal. Thus throughout history a struggle which is the same in its main outlines recurs over and over again."

I will finish this article when I get back from trying to recoup the $5.00 I lost to my 'cheating' golf buddies on my last golf round. In the meantime, consider Orwell's comments about the Low and how it applies to Obama's 'Fair Share' mantra. Perhaps the concepts of 'Fair Share' and 'Equality' are being used as bait by the Obama administration, as they have been used throughout history to gain power and deceive those most vulnerable. Obama's use of the uninformed plays right into the waiting arms of 'Big Brother' as they wait for him to give them their 'fair share.'

# 36

# A Deadly Label

Are our reporters exercising their First Amendment rights and responsibilities now in danger? At least one Fox News reporter has already been classified as a 'co-conspirator,' a name that labels him a criminal. Can the government assign a label to a person, any American citizen, and take action based on that label?

During questioning on March 5, 2013, Attorney General Eric Holder stopped short of entirely ruling out a drone strike against an American citizen on U.S. soil without trial. Holder's comment came in a letter to Sen. Rand Paul. Paul who had sent a letter to President Obama's CIA director nominee John Brennan asking for the administration's views on the president's power to authorize lethal force.

In his letter, Holder said, "It is possible, I suppose, to imagine an extraordinary circumstance in which it would be necessary and appropriate under the Constitution and applicable laws of the United States for the President to authorize the military to use lethal force within the territory of the United States." On March 7

Holder responded to pressure for a clearer answer. "It has come to my attention that you have now asked an additional question: 'Does the President have the authority to use a weaponized drone to kill an American not engaged in combat on American soil?' The answer to that question is no."

Again, this is another event where the Obama administration sees nothing, knows nothing, is conscious of nothing, and is not responsible for anything that seems not in their favor. Judging from the events happening, and Holder's responses, is there anything to prevent the Obama administration from taking their attack on American citizens one step further? If they can, at will, label a reporter doing his duty as a "co-conspirator" - can they not just as easily label someone they consider a serious threat to the Obama administration as an "enemy combatant?" According to Holder's explanation, that person could then be subjected to lethal force with a 'Drone strike' or by any other action necessary to eliminate the combatant threat.

The Obama administration continues to be seriously dangerous to our liberty. Otherwise, why would they continue to give evasive answers - or no answers at all?

# 37

# Fear Factor

We have all heard the term 'Big Brother' and generally understand the meaning of that concept. I thought I knew what it meant but had never given it much thought, except the idea that it referred to a government system of total control of a population. Recently, while at the library, I spotted the book '1984' by George Orwell, at a book sale and was reminded of 'Big Brother.' I bought the 'Signet Classic' version for fifty cents and thought I might look through it one day. I just started reading it and am surprised how closely the scenario seems to the trend developing in our country - and the world.

Although I am only about one-third through it, the concept is built around the condition of fear suffered by a man named Winston. He and others live in total fear that instantly they could be eliminated, either by public hanging or by simply disappearing. Some return later, and some do not. There is such fear to human interaction that people are afraid to look at each other directly in the eyes; afraid of how the 'Thought Police' might interpret certain eye contact. It's a book of total fear of the government - led by 'Big Brother.' And, with current events happening all around us today, no one who warns that 'Big Brother' is growing all around us should be considered an alarmist by those who refuse to look those people directly in the eyes. What are some signs? There are many, but for space and time, I will present only the most obvious ones.

First, is our federal government, itself. When anyone, at any level, is questioned about anything, they know nothing, or will have to "look into it and get back with you." Barack Obama wasn't 'in the loop' of that activity; Eric Holder doesn't know the answer; and to Hillary Clinton, "What difference, at this point, does it make!" Miller, from the IRS, knew nothing about anything. All his blatant arrogance could offer to Congressional questioning was, "I don't know."

A government unwilling to answer to the public most likely is a government to be feared and a government hiding something. Why are they afraid to offer truth to citizens? 'Big Brother' said simply, "Listen and obey."

Second is, of course, the IRS. If Obamacare continues to be implemented by the IRS they will know everything about everybody. It will be a 'Big Brother' computer. And, I predict that computer will one day have eye imprints that can identify a person with cameras located throughout the world. Big Brother will know where you are and what you are doing at all times. There will be no privacy - only fear. Most likely, that massive information center now being built in Utah will be the gathering site for all that information. It has that much storage and processing capacity - to gather information about every person on earth; and who they are talking to.

My next blog will continue this discussion. The topics will be the growing fear of criticizing Obama, and things like, 'what happened to Seal Team Six.'

# 38

# By The Book

I'm still reading the book, '1984' by George Orwell, where the concept of Big Brother is described. The more I read, the more familiarities I discover between conditions described in the book and conditions building in the Obama administration. I'm only a little way into the book, and two things specifically stand out as strong similarities.

First, is how Big Brother, in the book, has gained total control over everyone. It goes so far as interpreting people's thoughts with what is described as 'facespeak.' Thought Police and their ready accomplices are everywhere watching to see who is - and who is not - supporting Big Brother. Even answers to simple questions put people at risk of disappearing - or facing outright hanging. How can this be compared to things happening today?

Have you heard about the new questions asked during a doctor visit? Specifically: Do you own a weapon? Do you have any negative feelings? Do you ever feel stressed or depressed? It seems the IRS is being prepared to monitor results of these answers along with everything else about every single citizen. Oh, how easy it will be for them to know your spending habits, your preferences for everything and who your associates are.

A combination of all these things will give 'Big Brother' a clue as to what you are thinking. The 'Thought Police' shall have arrived.

Second, is the similarity to Obama's constant theme to perpetuate class warfare - separating the rich people from the poor people. Obama's mantra is taken directly from page 63 of this book. Quoting from a children's history textbook, Winston writes:

" - But in among all this great poverty there were just a few great big beautiful houses that were lived in by rich men who had as many as thirty servants to look after them. These rich men were called capitalists. They were fat, ugly men with wicked faces, like the one in the picture on the opposite page. - The capitalists owned everything in the world, and everyone else was their slave."

How can anyone even pretend Obama is not trying to create a new 'Big Brother' environment? It's already been written. He is simply following the planned scenario. Obama is doing the very same thing described in this quote from Orwell's book.

Obama will not step down at the end of his elected term. I believe 'Operation Fast and Furious' and our southern borders will play a significant part in this Obama takeover. Have you ever heard of 'Martial Law?'

# 39

# Action Security Force

In his 'Call to Service' speech on July 2, 2008 in Colorado Springs, then presidential candidate Barack Obama said, "We cannot continue to rely on our military in order to achieve the national security objectives we've set. We've got to have a civilian national security force that's just as powerful, just as strong, just as well-funded."

What did he mean by that? What would be the purpose of that civilian national security force? He has never explained, but recent events suggest he is beginning to act on that plan he revealed during that speech. Perhaps his new group, 'Organizing for Action' will be the driving force for that plan. The purpose for that new 'Obama support group' has still not been defined.

'Organizing for Action,' as it's now called, has not yet filed for tax-exempt status. Officials with the group say they are only in their fourth month of existence and federal law says it has two years to file paperwork with the IRS, though they plan on operating in the same manner as the targeted groups.

"In carrying out its work, OFA will operate as a 'social welfare' organization within the meaning of section 501(c)(4) of the Internal Revenue Code," the group's website states. But the nature of tax-exempt political groups is complicated when it comes to the IRS, experts say. The specific designation that tea party groups who were targeted applied for is called 501(c)(4), a loosely defined category that's existed since the tax code's 1913 creation.

"They have never been really clearly defined; they are supposed to do something called social welfare for the people of the community," says Fran Hill, professor at the University of Miami School of Law. "Then the IRS began to interpret social welfare as too difficult to interpret so they began to call 501(c)(4) a catchall and so anything that didn't fit anywhere else but they thought was kinda, sorta okay they would just shove into 501(c)(4)."

Who will be members of Obama's proposed civilian national security force? Will it be part of what's now the Homeland Security force? Homeland Security has ordered over 1.6 billion rounds of ammunition. Is it for Obama's new civilian national security force that's not yet presented itself? Or, could para-military Islamists now training in Latin American countries be part of his planned 'security force' sometime in the future? Perhaps he should explain - while he's trying to explain all his other unconstitutional and irrational activities.

# 40

# Secure Borders

Are our southern borders important? Do Americans need to know the connections with our southern borders, what's happening with Muslim insurgent training in Latin America, and "Operation Fast and Furious" concerning guns - lost and unaccounted-for high-power weapons?

Obama declared 'executive privilege' to prevent Eric Holder from giving more information to Congress about this gun program. That was several months ago. Has Congress forgotten about that program? Don't they realize the danger it represents? To me, it's at least as important as the other things Obama's administration is trying to answer now, in the news - now that the major news outlets have felt touched with Obama's treachery by attacking their AP services. Consider this news bulletin from a Kuwaiti City newspaper:

"KUWAIT CITY, Al-Seyassah Daily, April 28: "Iran's Revolutionary Guard is allegedly training a large number of Kuwaitis, Bahrainis and Saudis in a private training camp located in Waheera, a remote area near the borders of Venezuela and Columbia, and intends to use them to carry out terrorist activities within their respective countries and other areas across the world in case Iran is attacked militarily, Al-Seyassah Daily quoted a reliable source as saying.

The trainees are first sent to Venezuelan capital Caracas or Columbian capital Bogota via Damascus and from there, they are sent to the border region in cars, one of the militants who broke away from the Iranian group told the Daily."

Reportedly, the training camp is run by some Iranian intelligence officers and others affiliated to the Revolutionary Guard in cooperation with Hezbollah and Hamas. The trainees were given courses in making bombs, carrying out assassinations, kidnaping people and transporting the hostages to other locations.

The trainees have been trained to act in case there is a war against Iran. As per the plan, all embassies of Gulf countries, Egypt, Morocco and Jordan in Latin American countries were to be targeted. These bombings, however, will not be carried out by Iranian Shiites, but mercenaries from poorer countries like Venezuela, Columbia, Ecuador and Bolivia besides some other supporters from Hamas and other individuals so that Iranian involvement won't even be suspected. Drug smuggling to support this program has been linked to Hezbollah and Iran. It was also reported that, "Iran's proxies have been in the region for enough time to pose a cross-border threat to the U.S. in retaliation for any Israeli Strike.

Our southern borders, insurgents, terrorists, and lost weapons on our southern borders are important. And, any of the wrong combination of these could be dangerous to American citizens. Why is Barack Obama refusing to allow Eric Holder to give that information to Congress - and to American citizens? Isn't his first duty as a president to protect American lives and American citizens? Perhaps his action during the Benghazi event demonstrates his real concern for American lives - none.

# 41

# Dangerous Activity

Hardly a week has passed during the past several months that I have not had a blog entry on the implications and dangers regarding two events the Obama administration has been involved in - and has remained too secretive about. Those two topics have been about the Benghazi event and "Operation Fast and Furious," which is perhaps the most important and the most dangerous. Consequently, I firmly believe Obama continues to be a danger to the freedoms given us in our Constitution.

Finally, Obama's real character is beginning to be revealed. Whistle-blowers have come forward to expose the Benghazi event. Our government lied, then tried a cover-up. I believe the purpose for the event itself goes even deeper than that. Why was Ambassador Stevens there in that volatile zone?

Now, even more deceits, cover-ups and actions against our Constitution by the Obama administration are being revealed. Although he claims, "It wasn't me!" It was nevertheless his disregard and expressed disdain for our Constitution that allowed or encouraged those dangerous actions to occur. At one time he even said in certain words, that the Constitution gets in the way of some things he wanted to do. Regarding Benghazi, what was he doing that night after he had been briefed on that activity - other than preparing for a fund-raising trip to Las Vegas?

But, what about "Fast and Furious?" This forgotten event is perhaps the most dangerous of all. IT MUST NEVER BE FORGOTTEN!

On January 2, 2011, I released my book, 'America 20XX: The New World Order,' which gave a scenario of drug cartels helping Muslim insurgents preposition weapons in the desert near Casa Grande, Arizona. On January 28, 2011, only 26 days later, border agents found an Iranian book titled, "In Memory Of Our Martyrs," in that same desert near Casa Grande. What happened to those weapons - and perhaps many more? Why was that book found there? I wrote that novel as fiction, wondering if my concepts were even logical. New reports suggest perhaps they could have been very logical.

As reported in a new book, 'The War of All The People,' by Jon Perdue, the drug cartels and Islamofaschist terrorists have now forged an alliance not seen since the 70s or 80s. "The purpose for this activity is so that Iran can unleash terror on countries that support Israel in case Israel leashes an attack against Iran to stop its nuclear threat." According to Perdue, "Iran's proxies have been in the region for enough time to pose a cross-border threat to the U.S. in retaliation for any Israeli strike."

# 42

# His Oath

My current research indicates that the Muslim Brotherhood is a consortium to destroy everything non-Muslim on the face of the earth. It's written in their doctrine. The Saudi king, who pretends to be a bystander to the Islamic revolution, is actually one of the main players to clandestinely overthrow Western ideology and civilization. That includes American citizens.

Is Barack Obama, who has taken an oath to protect and defend the Constitution of the United States; and whose first and primary function as commander-in-chief is to protect American citizens, part of that conspiracy? Are his actions against American ideology intentional or simply a sign of arrogance and incompetence?

He could easily demonstrate his patriotism to the United States of America by promoting our domestic resources, by allowing more fossil fuel development in the United States and its surrounding waters. Instead, he and his administration have a direct policy and plan to penalize and execute anyone who tries.

Instead, he continues to buy that same fossil fuel from Saudi Arabia, and other countries that vow to destroy us. He bows to their Saudi king  then funds their plan to help them destroy us. Obviously, he was well trained in 'Islamic Taqiyya' while he was in Kenya and Indonesia.

And, how is he further assisting Saudi Arabia in their devious plans to destroy us? According to a new report:

"Saudi Arabia, the nation which produced 15 of the 19 hijackers in the 9/11 attacks, is about to become one of a handful of countries whose travelers can bypass normal passport controls at major U.S. airports. Sources tell the Investigative Project on Terrorism that this will mark the first time that the Saudi government will have a direct role in vetting who is eligible for getting fast-tracked for entry into the United States.

Homeland Security Secretary Janet Napolitano announced the agreement in January after meeting with Saudi Interior Minister Prince Mohammed bin Nayef. It 'marks another major step forward in our partnership,' Napolitano said at the time. 'By enhancing collaboration with the Government of Saudi Arabia, we reaffirm our commitment to more effectively secure our two countries against evolving threats while facilitating legitimate trade and travel.'"

While Saudi Arabia, the leader of the Muslim Brotherhood, secretly schemes with others to destroy America and the Western World we throw the doors wide open to help them. Is that any safer than picking up six rattlesnakes with two bare hands?

# 43

# His Arrogance

I've posted a comment similar to this before, but after listening to some of the Benghazi hearings, yesterday, I feel even more convinced of my first feelings about the incident. Strongly, I believe Barack Obama cares more about his status and his legacy than he does about the lives and personal safety of individual Americans. Barack Obama cares only about Barack Obama.

Can the world and his supporters forget so quickly that while American heroes were being slaughtered in Benghazi (and he knew it was happening because Leon Panetta said he told the president on the phone while it was happening) he went to bed and got a good night's sleep for his fund-raising trip to Las Vegas the next day? What was Barack Obama thinking while he was telling his supporters what a great president he would be for all Americans?

Smoke had not cleared from the ambassador's death trap while Obama was smiling, and feeding his campaign line to his uncaring supporters. What kind of man would do something like that? What kind of people would swear total allegiance and blind following to this kind of man? How can they consider themselves real

Americans - when they couldn't care less what happens to their fellow Americans who are being slaughtered while the president seeks only his self-fulfillment? He claims to be supporting the poor and middle-class, but at the same time he ignores American working-class and American patriots who give their lives for this great nation.

My greatest disappointment, however, is not with Barack Obama. I know his character - it's no better than that. It's what I expect from the deceiver who one day will become the 'beast,' that last antichrist. The indicators flow all around him. And, I'm not disappointed with the actions and lies of Hillary Clinton. Her character is no higher than that either. She was probably the most guilty of wrong-doing or incompetence in guiding that event. Her whole focus is on her status, not on individual American lives - American hero lives.

Since I'm a retired military officer, I understand the responsibility of the military in events such as this. The military had the capability to intervene in the Benghazi slaughter - maybe not stop it in time, but to at least show what America stands for. They could have saved some of those slaughtered toward the end of the event. My greatest disappointment is with General Martin Dempsey, the chairman of the joint chiefs of staff.

As senior officer of the military he should have forced defensive action to be taken to protect American lives. Of course, he had to follow the orders of the president and the secretary of defense, Leon Panetta, but if they gave a contradictory order to what's right, he should have immediately resigned.

A senior military officer should never support such an obvious evil. That evil should be left to people like Barack Obama. Martin Dempsey, come forward and say what happened - or support our Constitution with your resignation.

# 44

# His Endless Term

Okay, here I go again with another conspiracy theory about Barack Obama. My deepest gut instincts tell me the man will not give up the presidency at the end of his elected term. I hope and pray my feelings are totally wrong, but I'm still researching considering the possibility my instincts might be correct. Of course the major question is: how could that happen? It would take many complicated actions to facilitate that major event.

I've just begun, but already some interesting coincidences are exposing themselves. It begins with Obama's new organization called: Organizing for Action. When this group was recently formed, it was suggested that major donors to the group would be included as part of frequent meetings at the White House. Of course, the administration played that down, but did not say directly that it would not occur. Jay Carney used words to say it might occur under certain conditions. This new organization under its charter cannot campaign for Obama, but it can support Obama's goals.

The plan of the organization is to have a group in each of the fifty states, and according to one of the proposed ideas is to give financial and other support to members of both parties who support Obama's goals. One example given is that this organization will support John McCain since McCain is supporting Obama's gun control initiatives. The plan is to defeat other elected officials if they are opposed to Obama's plans. Isn't this interesting, since states will have to be involved to change the amendment that allows presidents to serve only two terms - or ten years total. Just imagine how much power these fifty units will have, especially if they have great financial support.

Speaking of financial support, there is also an interesting connection with the man who intends to buy America, using Obama as his puppet. Is there a connection to George Soros in all this activity? Absolutely! That connection is through a man named Erik Smith. Who is Erik Smith?

Erik Smith is now one of the board members of Obama's new group. The others are: Jim Messina, Stephanie Cutter, Robert Gibbs, Jennifer O'malley-Dillon, Julianna Smoot, and David Plouffe. David Axelrod, the Communist associate of Obama and his chief advisor, Valerie Jarrett, considers himself a consultant to the new group. Anyway, Erik Smith ran George Soros's Media Fund, and is now the executive for the Common Purpose Project, also largely funded by Soros. The lines are rapidly coming together.

# 45

# Ideals and Principles

Maybe - just a little maybe - it's possible that some degree of justice might be done about the Benghazi event. New information is finally easing out from those who were involved who are courageous enough to come forward. But, then there's the question: what is justice in the Benghazi event? Maybe, at this point, justice might be simply getting to the real truth of what happened, and why. For the four people who were murdered, there probably will never be real justice. Our government, our State Department, and our military leaders let them down - abandoned them to be slaughtered - disregarded all principles of what it means to be 'American.' Why?

When I was in the military; honor, duty, and country had special meanings. All military people were automatically possessed with those ideals, largely because we knew our leaders were guided by those principles. Now that the president, the previous secretary of defense, and the current chairman of the joint chiefs of staff make superficial excuses for not trying to protect those four Americans in harms way on an American mission, what will happen to those guiding ideals and principles?

The current secretary of defense exhibits even less patriotic character. He has never said anything positive about the United States. When questioned about the Benghazi event, Hillary Clinton threw up her hands and exclaimed, "At this point, what difference does it make!" Are these the actions and comments of what we deserve from American leadership?

Our military men and women voluntarily join to serve and protect the United States of America. When they join, their hearts and minds are totally dedicated to that great cause. Hopefully, those great heroes can maintain that level of diligence and patriotism within themselves even as they are led by those who exhibit character and principles alien to America's guiding principles.

(What do I know about military principles and what was a land of opportunity? In 1957, I left a 3-acre cotton patch in central Mississippi and joined the U.S. Air Force. During the next five years, I served as an enlisted medic and achieved the rank of only an E-4 , Airman First Class. During that time, however, I attended night college courses and completed college correspondence courses. Along the way, I applied for Officer Candidate School (OCS) and was accepted into the last class, graduating in June, 1963.

During the next few years, I completed my college degree and reached the rank of major before I decided to retire - at age 39. I was offered the opportunity to attend an advanced degree program when I submitted my retirement papers - which meant I was scheduled for more promotions. I had already made other plans, and declined the offer. I was satisfied with what I had already accomplished from that 3-acre cotton patch.

This should explain why I am so disgusted with

Obama and his administration. He encourages young people to 'wait for their fair share.' He doesn't encourage anyone to look at the great opportunities in America, and work hard to earn enough to contribute back to society. He encourages them to 'take' not to 'contribute.' In my opinion, Obama is concerned only about Obama.)

# 46

# Devious or Incompetent

I wish I knew. I wish I knew for sure if two incidents that took place in the Obama administration were intentionally dangerous, conspiratorial, or just plain and simple incompetence. But, if the whole world acknowledges and respects Obama's great and superior intelligence, then one must assume the actions I'm concerned about would not be from incompetence or ignorance. These are the activities surrounding 'Operation Fast and Furious' and the incident in Benghazi. If these events did not occur from simple incompetence, then one must assume they were intentional and devious.

Many high-powered weapons were lost from a questionable and weird program to track weapons to determine their destination and their use. Eric Holder refused to answer important questions regarding this program, and after a long time it seems that event has been forgotten. The implausible situation here is that they were trying to track weapons without any tracking devices or methods to track them. As a result, an American hero was murdered with one of the weapons.

The dark question surrounding this event is what happened to all those other unaccountable weapons? Making this question even more important is the question: why is our government buying billions of rounds of ammunition? Are those weapons and that ammunition to be combined one day to create danger to American citizens?

And, questions about the Benghazi incident should never be abandoned. It seems, at the moment, there is a renewed interest in finding those answers. It seems some people who were involved are trying to come forward to give some answers but they are afraid of repercussions from the Obama administration if they give any details to explain what really happened and the ability of our forces to intervene. Why all the secrecy to deny the truth to come out. Why is the Obama administration threatening anyone who comes forward to give pertinent information?

We are American citizens. It's our right to know what happened to our fellow citizens - and why. What is our government hiding? Why are they hiding so many activities. Didn't Obama say his would be the most transparent administration in our history. Does he understand what the word 'transparent' means?

# 47

# CSCOPE is no Joke

More subtle and hidden danger to America and our democracy. Have you heard of CSCOPE? It's an education program now being used and expanded in Texas. However, according to comments by our government, it will likely be expanded and required in all states. According to its promoters, it's not really a curriculum, it's a method of lesson presentation.

So, what kind of presentations are made in the curriculum (oops) lesson plans under CSCOPE? Just some examples: The Boston Tea Party members were terrorists; Christopher Columbus was dangerous to our eco-system; Fairness is more important than freedom and options. These are only a few of the examples. Many more examples are there, but are not available for public view. Why?

Why? Teachers are forced to implement CSCOPE into their classroom teaching. And, they must sign a document saying they will not reveal contents of the lesson plans to parents or anyone outside the closed CSCOPE system. You don't believe this? You can research and find that some teachers have already been fired in Texas because they disclosed some of the information to parents! This is no joke. It's a dangerous threat to our democracy.

From my recent research, I must make two conclusions about CSCOPE. First, it undoubtedly must be funded and promoted by a Muslim country or a Muslim consortium - probably Obama's friends, the Muslim Brotherhood. That source most likely is Saudi Arabia or another Sharia Wahabi group. They already have their hands in many of our education programs. Second, it's another subtle movement toward Agenda 21. Agenda 21 is the program ordinarily promoted as 'sustainable development.' This is a plan to consolidate and centralize people to minimize the use of earth resources. This is moving closer to the concept of 'Big Brother' in George Orwell's book '1984.' I'm re-reading this book now.

But - what better should we expect from Obama and his administration? He said he was going to fundamentally change America. Can Americans survive that change?

# 48

# Reasons to Write

As any novel writer knows, it takes a lot of time, energy, and focus to write a novel, especially one longer than 100,000 words. Then it takes even as much time to do the editing and proofing. In summary, a fiction writer puts a lot of 'heart and soul' into writing.

And, when a fiction writer tries to use current events, either political or social, to structure the concept, this takes even more time and research - more 'heart and soul.' Such was the case with my two most recent novels: 'America 20XX: The New World Order,' and '666: Mark of the Beast.' My intention was not only to create an interesting and entertaining read, but also to present two 'what if' scenarios concerning things happening around us.

In the case of America 20XX, my goal was to, while creating an interesting read, also create an answer to the question: how would or could a corrupt government take over our country and turn it into something our forefathers warned us about. My research and focus suggested to me that the two most important criteria to accomplish that were to quietly eliminate influential opponents, either by election fraud or planned accidents, and to confiscate personal weapons.

The concept of '666' was to present a 'what if' situation that would allow a leader of a one-world government to emerge. Further, to show if that were to happen it would be the fulfillment of biblical prophesy that would put Israel in grave danger - thereby putting the whole world in peril. It would be the beginning of the Apocalypse. I had to read the book of Revelation many, many times to prepare for these scenes. That's why many of my posts are related to these Revelation prophesies.

A little tidbit emerges each time Revelation is read. That's why my novel-in-progress will be more extensive. It will begin the Revelation story from the defeat at Troy. Would you believe - the ancient site of troy is only about 100 miles from the seven biblical churches described in the Book of Revelation.

# 49

# Attack on Christians

I thought I would share this since it seems to be a common and growing attitude within our great nation. From my perspective, more and more people are turning from - and even mocking - Christianity more and more. Now, it seems to be even more currently fashionable to criticize Christians, and even accuse them of being radicals. That attitude is fulfilling Biblical prophesy. At the extreme end, according to Revelation 13 verse 18, the time will come when those who refuse to worship the other god will even be beheaded. The Bible describes that other god as the 'strange god.'

The following is a letter to the editor I am submitting to my local newspaper in response to other letters and comments. I have to wait until May because I have already submitted my April submission. This is that letter:

"You Christians and your god! You people are spiraling out of control now that America has woke up and put you in your place." This is an online comment from msfreethinker, one of a few people brave enough to make attack comments, but not brave enough to use their real names. This attack was against Mike Fullilove and his April 22 letter, "Why are we messing with marriage?"

These online attacks have become so repetitious and boring they serve no purpose, other than weird self entertainment. It seems they try to see who can be the most boastful with their superior knowledge and use of derogatory names. I usually earn a new descriptive name each time I submit a letter. (Added for this blog entry: I usually go a little overboard in my letters just to incite them more just to see how far they will go with their vicious attacks and name-calling. Maybe it's my weird form of entertainment.)

However, this response, "You Christians and your god!" opens a new light to a serious problem - the attack on Christianity. Perhaps msfreethinker and others like him or her might take a new look at Christianity and ponder the implications of a Christian prophesy made 2000 years ago - that can only be understood in today's world. Revelation, Chapter 13, verses 13-18 gives that modern clue. How did Apostle John know about rockets, missiles, and lasers bringing fire from the sky? How did he know about computers and holograms making an image speak? How did he know about RFID chips that could be placed in one's right hand?

Maybe msfreethinker should read, consider, and interpret more. Maybe one day he or she might be blessed enough to become one of "You Christians."

# 50

# A Reason for Guns

I've read several blogs lately in different forums that question our Founders' intentions of the Second Amendment. In many of those blogs, the writers suggest our Founders never knew weapons would become so powerful and fast, as with repeating rifles and high-capacity ammunition clips. At the time that amendment was considered, there were only muzzle-loading rifles, pistols, and cannons.

Those blog-writers suggest that today, with more powerful weapons, our Founding Fathers would never pass such an amendment. These anti-gun writers totally miss the point of the Second Amendment. Those who wrote and enacted that amendment were not thinking about ownership of weapons for hunting and target practice. The amendment was designed for personal protection, family protection, and to defend our country from all enemies - foreign and domestic. Could a muzzle-loader do that today? Only if those who mean to do us harm have only muzzle-loaders.

Our Founding Fathers should have gone even further with the Second Amendment. Instead of permitting ownership of firearms, they should have made it mandatory that every competent citizen must own a firearm. Of course, there would still be murder, there would still be armed robbery, and there would still be mayhem. But, before one committed those heinous acts they would have to consider if their lives were in danger. It would be a reasoning point for every armed evil person. Consider how the world might be different if historically every citizen were required to own a weapon.

Would Vladimir Lenin have been able to subdue Russians, murder thousands, then set a standard for his successor, Joseph Stalin, to annihilate millions more in his purge of dissidents if all citizens had owned weapons? Would Adolph Hitler have been able to conquer Germany with only a few 'Brown Shirts' if all German citizens had owned weapons? Then he killed millions - without even a whimper from those innocent and unarmed victims. Pol Pot killed millions of Cambodia's citizens at his leisure since none were allowed to own weapons. At a moment's whim he killed anyone of status and anyone who expressed any disagreement. How could these innocent victims of these three major events defend themselves or their country? They had no weapons.

Unfortunately, weapons are dangerous and cause tragedy to hundreds and even thousands of innocent victims. However, without defensive weapons the loss could be millions of innocent victims and the loss of a country. Loss of a country too often means the loss of everything.

Two of my novels: 'America 20XX: The New World Order,' and '666: Mark of the Beast' are written on the concept of banning personal weapons. What are Obama's plans?

# 51

# The Antichrist

In a previous entry I wrote that there are, and will be, many antichrists who come forth throughout the world to deceive us. I also stated that the most dangerous antichrist, the beast, will not assign himself to that role. Satan will choose him and assign him those great powers when Satan chooses. Now that person does not know he will become the End Times antichrist. This is according to Revelation, Chapter 13, the first two verses:

"And I stood upon the sand of the sea, and saw a beast rise up out of the sea, having seven heads and ten horns, and upon his horns ten crowns, and upon his heads the name of blasphemy.

2, And the beast which I saw was like unto a leopard, and his feet were as the feet of a bear, and his mouth as the mouth of a lion: and the dragon gave him his power, and his seat, and great authority." (Earlier, I also gave my interpretation of these descriptive traits.)

At this time, that person continues to build his power base thinking he's doing great things for mankind. He will get his full power, and that assignment to be that beast, that antichrist, when the seven continents, the seven heads, are combined under one rule. I just found another reference which indicates this possibility even more. This is also in Revelation: Chapter 17, verses 12-14:


"And the ten horns which thou sawest are ten kings, which have received no kingdom as yet; but receive power as kings one hour with the beast." "These have one mind, and shall give their power and strength unto the beast." "These shall make war with the Lamb, and the Lamb shall overcome them:"


Very interesting. I have no interpretation other than a description of a 'One World Order.' One person will lead ten nations to attack Israel. I have made my ideas well known whom I think that leader will be - at the appointed time.


# 52

# Too Much Information

I just watched a program on Fox News about a new data center NSA (National Security Agency) is building in the Utah desert south of Salt Lake City. The purpose for the facility is to collect data, supposedly gazillions of gigabits. Of course all the information is not available, since it's a secret facility, but enough information is available to make the idea of something that capable of monitoring everyone on earth certainly scary. Ever hear of George Orwell's 'Big Brother?'

According to the program, data will be collected from phones, computers, smart phones, I-pads, and anything that can transmit a data signal. And, it can monitor every signal from every person on earth no matter the transmission devise. The facility is being built now, and it will be larger than the Pentagon when it's finished. Of course, the purpose will begin as something positive to protect the United States, and humanity. But, things evolve to their highest and most profound use - if controlled by someone who wants to do 'just a little more' of the facility capability. Little things always grow into big things. Then, we lose our freedom.

Isn't total information just one step away from total surveillance and control? With a world central monitoring station, such as that NSA facility, wouldn't it be every easy and simple to also send signals from that facility. And, what if those signals were sent to RFID chips implanted into people? And, what if that procedure started very harmlessly, such as gathering personal data for health purposes and medical care. That's reasonable. Then, what if they added another application that would serve as a credit or debit card? That sounds reasonable - doesn't it? Suddenly, before we are aware of what's happening we have the 'Mark of the Beast' as described in Chapter 13 of the Book of Revelation upon us.

Of course we all know the only purpose of our government, especially the Obama administration, is to protect us. But wait! What about those lost weapons from 'Operation Fast and Furious?' What about the protection they gave to the four Americans slaughtered in Benghazi?

Did Orwell see the future in his book (1984) when he wrote about 'Big Brother' watching? Perhaps Orwell didn't see the whole future.

# 53

# Early Changes

Have you heard of the CSCOPE common core curriculum being used by many schools to be eligible for more funding and grants from Obama's 'Race to the Top' education plan? In some Texas schools the curriculum and lesson plans from that common core curriculum were intentionally kept secret from parents until some parents got legislators involved to investigate that program. Their investigation learned that many of the lessons included positive values of Islam, and negative values of Christians and ordinary citizens.

Now, add this intentional degradation of our American values taught in American classrooms to Obama's new emphasis on Pre-K education. It's one of the items he's focusing on to demand more money in his current proposed budget. Referring to Pre-K means assigning children to classrooms before kindergarten age. That means ages 3 and 4. Many children are still wetting their pants at that age. Why would Obama want to start brainwashing them at that earlier age - and separate them from their parents who are the ones most responsible for teaching basic understanding of life to their children at that age?

Most normal people know what children need at that age - and it's not to learn algebraic equations. They first need to learn how to be people - people who understand life and appreciate other people. I believe these actions he keeps implementing suggest more danger ahead for our great nation.

Continuing with my 'conspiracy theories' I believe Obama is continuing with his plan to 'fundamentally change' America. That's what he said he was going to do when he campaigned for president. Many believed that 'fundamental change' referred to freedom and prosperity. I never did - and I still don't. I believe his fundamental change is to move America further away from those things traditional Americans have always valued most - freedom and individual opportunity to develop to one's highest aspirations.

He's beginning that transformation with our 3 and 4 year old children. Doesn't that sound familiar to what happened somewhere overseas in the 1930s-1940s? Barack Obama will not give up the presidency at the end of this current term!

# 54

# Robbing the Poor

Barack Obama's policies continue to prey on the poor and middle-class - especially the most poor. Yet the poorest in our great nation continue to worship him even more - or should I say worship 'Him' even more?

I have submitted various forms of this blog before, but something happened to me yesterday that again caused me great concern for those who are unfortunate to have even less than I have been blessed to have. It concerned my lawn mower.

As I was mowing my lawn, my lawnmower suddenly started coughing and sputtering, and struggled to make the next engine stroke. Finally, it just died. One might think it was out of gas, but I had just filled the tank. That happened a few months ago, so at that time I called someone to fix the lawnmower. The repair bill was $98, and the technician told me to buy only enough gas for one time to mow the lawn.

Of course, I used the smallest container to buy gas - 2-gallons- and didn't think about it anymore - until it quit this time. So, being at least reasonably aware, I drained the gas tank and bought some ethanol-free gasoline at a nearby store that sells it. Guess what? My lawnmower runs like new - for the first time in many years!

My first thought was, "Thank Goodness, I don't have to pay another $98!" My very next thought was, "I wonder how many people who can't afford that $98 have to do without other things if they have to have their small engines repaired - especially lawnmowers. But, small engines are used for many items such as blowers, outboard motors, motorcycles, pressure cleaners and emergency generators. How many poor people have been stripped of precious funds due to ETHANOL? And, now Obama wants to increase it from 10 percent to 15 percent. That's not to help poor people, as he claims - it's to subsidize his rich supporters!

Obama proudly proclaims his zeal to help the middle-class and poor in our society, but is that what he really has in mind? His speeches are all about helping those who have less than the evil rich people get their fair share. Yet, his actions are directly opposed to achieving that humanitarian goal. While he proudly and boastfully talks of putting more money in their front pockets, he steals even more from their wallets and bank accounts. He robs their few precious assets from them as he convinces them he is their savior that will give them more. How does this happen?

Most people not considered wealthy must put gasoline in their automobiles to get to work. Half of what they pay for gasoline is money that Obama's policies strips from their available assets. That's money that could be used for many other things that might help stimulate the economy.

I filled my two automobiles with gasoline this week. One is a Toyota with which I just returned from a trip to California. The round trip was about 5000 miles. I had left my older second car tank-empty in my garage. The Toyota sucked in $46.00 of gas, and the Buick inhaled

$49.00 worth. While I was putting gas in those cars, I was wondering how much of that money, and the $500 of gas I bought on the trip, was going to fund Islamic terrorists who want to kill Americans - including me!

I wonder how much of that approximately $600 worth of gas I bought went to pay someone to kill Americans. Needless to say, I became more irritated when I also considered how much of that money was wasted, thrown into the wind, because America does not have an energy policy that allows us to put that money back into our economy. Can you just imagine how active and viable our economy would be if only half of my gas money, and yours, went back into our domestic economy, instead of sending most of it to people who want to destroy us? If gas were $1.00 a gallon, look at all the billions that could be recycled for other goods and investments in America.

And, since I live on the Gulf Coast near New Orleans, I remember when the president stopped all oil drilling in the Gulf. Then he made loans and donations to Brazil to drill their oil when many of our drilling rigs went there, when he wouldn't allow them to operate in our waters. It makes one wonder who our American enemy really is. Our economic situation and our unemployment problem could easily be solved with just a sensible and patriotic energy policy. Let's drill our own oil, and treat is as a utility rather than as a commodity. In either case, don't let our enemies sell us oil that funds America's downfall.

Due to his energy policy of not allowing more oil drilling in and around the United States, gasoline prices have doubled since he became president in 2008. That's doubled! When he took office, gasoline was approximately $1.85 per gallon. At this moment, it's over $3.60 per gallon. That means people are penalized as much as $100.00 to $200.00 a month for gasoline - just to get to their jobs. And those needy people still consider Barack Obama their hero and savior? Obviously, once a savior is recognized, he is never questioned by his worshipers. How many miles-per-gallon are lost because of ethanol - 2, 3, 4? Is this not robbing many poor people? And he wants to increase ethanol to 15 percent! AND THEY STILL WORSHIP HIM?

# 55

# Penalizing the Poor

Obama's attack on American energy production has increased costs in every sector of the American economy, thereby penalizing the poor and middle-class the most. How? The answer is simple. The cost of energy determines the cost of almost everything in our modern society.

Electricity and power bills have increased for the average consumer because the president has curtailed available energy resources. The poor and middle-class have to pay more for electricity and heat, even if heated by other than electricity. With less production of coal, that cost has also increased, or those who had used coal for heating have had to convert to other heat sources. These increased energy costs are also suffered by businesses and factories who must also increase the cost of their products and services to remain in business. The falling domino effect runs the course until the final inflated costs reach the consumer - largely the poor and middle class who are hurt the worst. But, by keeping his finger pointed at the wealthy, Obama continues to be the savior of the poor and middle-class. They close their eyes as they fold their hands in prayer to him.

And, we should not forget the effects of ethanol. Although this was an active program long before Barack Obama was elected president, he still has done nothing to curtail its devastating effects. Let's consider just a few.

First, many people report engine problems with their automobiles from using ethanol. When ethanol was first introduced it was to support two needs; less reliance on oil, since at that time the oil price was beginning to escalate faster. And, the major purpose for its introduction was to be more environmentally friendly. This was partially in response to the 'climate change' promoters who were determined to make money with their great scare tactics. (Has Al Gore ever admitted how wealthy he became with his great 'save the world' environmental program?) Many engines are having to be repaired from the damage created by ethanol use.

Again, Barack Obama puts a dagger through the economic hearts of the poor and middle-class, who often can't afford those repairs. Yet, they continue to believe his promises that his sole purpose as president is to give them their 'fair share.' Could he mean a fair share of despair, not their fair share of the country's wealth?

Cost of repairing automobile engines however is not necessarily the greatest disaster created by the use of ethanol against the poor and middle-class. Often, that's a one-time cost that can be absorbed with payments on credit cards or by giving up some other family necessity. The greatest cost to those who can afford it least is the increased cost of food. Even the least wealthy must have food, and nowadays there are not enough personal gardens to fulfill that need. Only a few people now have a garden, a cow, chickens and pigs from which they can get their food. Most people now must buy their food from the grocery store. So, how does ethanol affect the price of food?

At this time, most ethanol is made from corn. Corn is also used many other ways, especially related to other food, many foods that one would not imagine as an added ingredient for improved taste, firming a product, color, or to create different blends of another food product. Corn is also used as a livestock food. In effect, corn is used in most things related to food and food production.

What happens when much of that corn product is transferred to produce ethanol? Have you noticed the price of food, lately? Are you aware that a gallon of milk has skyrocketed from $1.99 two years ago to over $4.00 today? Have you seen the price of beef, or has that price become so expensive you can no longer buy beef? Have you seen the price of any food product, and can say it has not increased in price at least 25 percent during the past two years?

Obama has increased the price of all food to a level that forces many to depend on food stamps for subsistence. That dependency increases his power and control over them - thereby making him their savior. Have they no sense of rationality? 'Are his worshipers really that gullible and stupid?

# 56

# Education is the Key

Before I became focused on the dangerous threat Barack Obama is to our great nation, I was more focused on researching and writing about the education dilemma in America and what we could do to improve it. Improving education effectiveness is not only helping students, individually, to become successful and productive, it's another link in the important chain to protect America.

A more educated society is certainly a society that can more easily recognize and interpret the dangers from within - such as exist today. With 30 percent of our students becoming disillusioned and dropping out of school, how can we expect to continue our great country at the level which it has existed all these years?

Last month I wrote a 'letter to the editor,' locally, expressing my concern about the waste of taxpayer money on the new rush to 'Pre-K' education. Two educators responded saying that my reference to justify my position was 'outdated.' This is a copy of the letter I just submitted in reply to that letter:

"In a previous letter, I wrote that Pre-K education is a futile endeavor that wastes taxpayer money. Two educators disagreed, and said the study I referenced was outdated. Strange - because it's the same study that's still the basis for current school integration, busing, and 'social capital' concepts and programs.

That study is the 'Equality of Educational Opportunity Survey,' called the 'Coleman Report,' named for Professor James Coleman. His survey was the largest ever conducted, over a two-year period beginning in 1964. It included over 4000 schools, 60,000 teachers, and 570,000 students. In 1966, the research team concluded, "the social class of the student body was the determining factor in education - not school curriculum or school quality." Coleman said, "Families make the difference, not schools." Their conclusion did not support the purpose for the survey, which was to prove that schools getting more funding were more successful.

Coleman's survey is the only objective major national education survey ever done. Current studies and surveys are now designed to prove a conclusion made before the survey. They are most often conducted by those with something to sell, such as curriculum developers or training programs - or those who want to create more jobs to get more taxpayers money.

From objective research, Pre-K education does help students to the third grade. After that, the family influence becomes the overbearing factor to education success. Drop-outs are our greatest education and social dilemma - 30 percent - not standardized test scores. Yet, society ignores this greater tragedy."

This irrational focus on standardized test scores is unfair to society, students, and especially teachers. Now, the emphasis on those standard tests encourage many teachers and administrators to 'cheat' just to keep their jobs. An example is what just happened to the superintendent and 35 educators in Atlanta. The comparative evaluation and grading system of educators is totally irrational. Competent research proves that grades are more determined by the local society and culture than by school tactics and techniques. For example: the ten states with the lowest scores and highest drop-out rates had an average poverty rate of 16 percent and a robbery rate of 1072 per 100,000 citizens. The ten states with the best education rates had a poverty rate of 10 percent and a robbery rate of 530 per 100,000.

If teachers are to be graded and judged on school performance it must be based on a scale that takes these local factors into consideration. Ordinarily, a teacher in a high poverty zone has no chance to produce the same results as a teacher in the lowest poverty zones. It's easy and convenient to condemn these 35 educators for cheating, but perhaps they were just trying to survive and keep their jobs.

# 57

# Attacking Christians

There's a group of 6 or 7 people in my local newspaper area who attack - viciously attack - anyone who mentions God or Jesus or Christians in a 'letter to the editor' or in a 'sound off' comment. These attackers are the ones who make their comments online responding to those published editorials. Most obviously are cowards, since they ordinarily use made-up phony names to remain hidden under rocks. Two were finally identified so they now use their real names - but their comments are just as insensitive, discourteous, and vicious. They exhibit the same attitude and approach that Obama does: ignore the message and attack the messenger. It happened in my local newspaper today regarding the TV program, 'The Bible,' so I was spurred to make a comment, especially to those who think the Bible is just a joke - one big fantasy story.

Saul of Tarsus (later Paul) was a Roman who persecuted Jews until he 'saw the light.' Then he became Paul of Tarsus and was beheaded in Rome for his Christian faith. Perhaps others can 'see the light' if they read and try to understand that reading a little further. And, there are several good clues. To keep this brief, I will just refer to the Book of Revelation, for now. Remember - it was written two thousand years ago.

The first verse of Chapter 13 says: "And I stood upon the sand of the sea, and saw a beast rise up out of the sea, having seven heads —." This is referring to the last beast, the last antichrist. John had no knowledge of 7 continents at that time. Jesus gave him that vision to show a combined world at the end times. Otherwise, how did John know there were 7 continents? John and other apostles wrote of 'the sea' referring to mankind or souls, but this reference was different. It included the word 'sand' to denote an actual body of water.

In verse 13, speaking of the second beast (the false prophet,) John wrote: "And he doeth great wonders, so that he maketh fire come down from heaven on earth in the sight of men." This is speaking of the end times, 2000 years ago. How did John know about rockets, missiles, and laser beams at that time? He saw those things in a vision, but he couldn't explain them in current terms.

Verse 15: "And he had power to give life unto the image of the beast, that the image of the beast should both speak, and cause that as many as would not worship the image of the beast should be killed." Again, this was written over 2000 years ago. How did John know about computers, keyboards, WIFI, and holograms? Christ gave John these visions - he did not explain the visions.

# 58

# Who's the Target?

I'm just sitting here listening to the rain and wondering which project I should start next. I put my big novel on hold three months ago to write the 'Obama Ring' book. The novel will be an action book probably titled, 'From Troy to Ephesus' and will give a fictional account of how the descendants of those who escaped the massacre at Troy were involved in the Christian events in Ephesus. I got a chapter (6000 words) finished before I started the Obama book.

Now, Obama's current actions have distracted me again. I'm wondering what the connection is between the 1.6 billion rounds of ammunition the DHS just bought and his new Action organization. My fiction instincts tell me there's some connection that will involve martial law after two years into his current term - so his current term will never have to end. Anything could be used for an excuse - gun laws, drug smugglers, or an event regarding North Korea or Israel. It could even be set off by an event such as the Branch Dividians (David Koresh) saga in 1993, where 83 men, women, and children died from government over-reaction. Could that happen again - on a larger scale? I still can't decide which to begin. It's still raining.

# 59

# Organizing for Action

Barack Obama has established a new political organization called, 'Organizing for Action.' Supposedly, the purpose for the organization is to push Obama's agenda, and to train future political supporters. This organization is established as a tax-free group. According to leaders of the group, it will be separate from the DNC and will not share funds with or support the DNC. An analysis in McClatchy News, yesterday, said the DNC and its followers are concerned this new Obama organization will siphon funds from their normal contributors. It will not be associated in any way with the Democratic Committee.

Jim Messina, Chairman of the new organization wrote, "We have a remarkable opportunity right now to change our country, and if we can take the enthusiasm and passion that people showed throughout the campaign and channel it into the work ahead of us, we will be unstoppable." He continued, "As the chair of Organizing for Action, I will be deeply involved in this new organization, but it will be organizers like you who will determine where it goes. I have no doubt we can take this grassroots movement to new and extraordinary heights."

Please note two comments he made. 1. "to change our country;" 2. "new and extraordinary heights." Perhaps he did not realize what dangerous thoughts these are. These words mean they intend to change America. The question is; in what direction? That answer is hard to comprehend, but I believe it's true. It means we are moving further away from democracy and freedom in America.

What makes this even more believable that Obama would disregard our constitution? On the 'Today' show in February, 2012, Obama said, "What's frustrated people is that I've not been able to implement every aspect of what I said in 2008. Well, it turns out our Founders designed a system that makes it more difficult to bring about change than I would like sometimes."

In my last two books: 'The Day America Died' and 'Obama's Ring: The Seat of Satan' I wrote that Obama will not give up leadership of America at the end of his elected term. Is it possible, and I firmly believe that it is, that this new group formed to support Obama is actually a group to explore ways to insure Barack Obama can continue in his position as President of the United States past the end of his elected term? I suppose Obama worshipers will love this idea; but what about our Constitution - and Freedom?

# 60

# Why I do This

Why do I put so much time and energy in posting these blogs about Obama that, to some, might appear alarmist and far-fetched? I've concluded there are two major reasons. Of course, there's always the possibility that I'm off my rocker and have an odd view of reality. And, if I were just writing off the top of my head I would seriously consider that possibility. Unfortunately, most of these alarmist things I write have much research and background to support those views - at least enough to make those things worthy of closer scrutiny.

So, let's begin with reason number one:

Do I really feel Obama and his administration threaten our democracy and our Western way of life? Absolutely! As an American citizen, am I responsible for trying to protect my country? Absolutely! When I joined the military, in 1957, I took an oath to defend my country against all enemies 'foreign and domestic' who threaten our way of life. My oath has not expired.

I see that threat, and now it's a combined threat both foreign and domestic. As I reported in an earlier blog, a prominent Muslim said there is 'an evil alliance' between the Obama administration and the Muslim

Brotherhood. The more I research, the more I uncover that 'evil alliance.' That evil alliance must be challenged so they realize there are many of us who still believe in American freedoms, and the responsibility of Americans to defend those freedoms. But, why me? That's the second reason.

Reason number two:

I've lived the American dream - and I want others who love this country to have the freedom to live the American dream. And, the American dream doesn't mean to wait on the sidelines and have promises of 'free stuff' fulfilled. It means the great feeling of accomplishment earned at the end of the day when you have done your best, when you have contributed something to society, and when you look up at the end of each day and say, "Thank You for making me the person I am." The American dream is to feel the satisfaction of rewards from a 'job well done.'

Why me? An older person, as I am at 74, has a greater duty other than to retire. If God has blessed us to have more and longer experiences it must be for a special reason. Perhaps that reason is to set the best example we can for those younger who look forward and question their future. They must see us demonstrating love and respect for our country - and humanity. We are free to do that.

Many younger people - today - are not free to express political opinions! It's too dangerous for many who must still work for a living to criticize Obama or his administration. Most who work for the government, and their numbers are growing, have had their free speech restricted and have been told not to criticize Obama or his followers. They must keep silent to protect their jobs so they can provide for their families and their future. They are not free to express their concern! We are. The worst that could happen to us is that the 'black helicopters' will show up on our lawn, and we will disappear. But - what the heck - it's been a long and good ride. We elders who have been so blessed must give others the same opportunity to have those same blessings.

# 61

# Who is the Enemy?

Our Founding Fathers recognized the possibility of a despotic and tyrannical government. They realized that unaware citizens could easily be deceived to support such a leader and such a government. That's why they said we must have the right to bear arms - to own weapons. They were not proposing weapons just for hunting game and target practice. They meant serious weapons to dispel a tyranny and to keep the United States free. But, perhaps they got the wording a little wrong with formation of the Second Amendment.

The words should have been, "All citizens 'MUST' bear arms to demonstrate their love of country and their determination to keep it free." If every competent citizen owned a serious firearm and understood the purpose for that ownership, it's unlikely a shot would ever have to be fired to maintain our freedom. The Barack Obamas of the world, and their determined friends the Muslim Brotherhood, wouldn't waste their time trying to conquer

America. They would stay in their own Islamic countries and continue to aimlessly slaughter each other - in the name of pure power control, and their Allah.

But, since we are now under this bold threat from Islamists who boast they 'will destroy our way of life' there are two questions we must consider. The first question is, 'How spellbinding is the influence of Obama's Seat of Satan ring on his coming plans and actions?" The second question is, "How many will be casualties identified in this Bible reference: Revelation, Chapter 20, Verse 4?"

In his 'Call to Service' speech July 2, 2008 in Colorado Springs, then presidential candidate Barack Obama said, "We cannot continue to rely on our military in order to achieve the national security objectives we've set. We've got to have a civilian national security force that's just as powerful, just as strong, just as well-funded." What did he mean by that? What would be the purpose of that civilian national security force? He has never explained, but recent events suggest he is beginning to act on that plan he revealed during that speech.

Recently, the Department of Homeland Security bought 1.6 billion (that's billion - with a B) rounds of high-powered ammunition including 450 million rounds of .40 hollow-point military style, 200 million rounds of .223 rifle ammunition, and 176,000 rounds of .308 168-grain hollow-point boat tail (HPBT) sniper ammunition. Comparing that to our usage in the Afghanistan war, it's enough to last 20 years. And there's more: 7000 full-auto assault rifles, and 2700 armored vehicles. There's still some uncertainty about the vehicles, but The Department of Homeland Security has not revealed the purpose for the other weaponry. (Hollow-point ammunition is not used for target practice. It expands and splits upon impact and is used to blow large holes in people.)

Is it to be used against drug smugglers crossing our southern borders? Is it to be used against radical jihadists led by the ghost of Osama Bin Laden wading ashore at the Boardwalk in Atlantic City? Or is to be used against those rowdy grandmothers who don't win enough when they play 'Bingo' at the community center? Who are these weapons to be used against? Our Founding Fathers spoke against a force such as this and said it would be dangerous to citizens - and democracy. Is it?

And, we still can't disregard the events that took place during 'Operation Fast and Furious,' where many AK-47s were lost - unaccounted for. Supposedly, they were destined for drug smugglers. But, was that the real purpose and destination? Obama does not say, and he uses 'Executive Privilege' to prevent the real information to be disclosed. Why all the secrecy about those 'lost' AK-47s?

And, very important; there must NEVER be universal gun registration. That would put a clear target on the backs of all legal gun owners.

# 62

# Obama's Muslim Friends

Perhaps the answer to what happened in Benghazi might give a clue to the peril the United States faces regarding Barack Obama's ideas for America and the world. Why did Obama allow four Americans to be slaughtered by Islamic radicals without showing any concern for their lives? There are three possible answers to this question:

First; Obama was afraid he would upset his Islamic cohorts. His friends might think he was no longer supporting them, in which case the Muslim Brotherhood had to be involved. He TOTALLY avoided calling them Islamists or radicals - until being forced to make a general reference - not a direct reference, much later. In my recent blog I reported that a prominent Muslim said the cooperation between America and Saudi Arabia (The Muslim Brotherhood) was an "evil alliance."

Second; a mission was underway that would expose an operation that Obama wanted to keep secret. If it were a secret mission, then normal procedure is to have a backup operations plan to prevent a catastrophe. Why didn't they execute the backup plan? The military would not act in a dangerous situation such as this event without a backup escape plan. If there were not a backup plan, then every senior person involved should be charged with dereliction of duty. I was in the military for 21 years; don't let anyone tell you otherwise. I was, in one assignment, the point contact for a serious backup plan. I know the military drill. And, where were the secretary of defense and the chairman of the joint chiefs staff when these activities were going on for MANY HOURS? They said they talked to the president one time that night, then nothing more was reported or discussed. Did they all wipe their hands of it and go to bed while four fellow Americans were being slaughtered?

Third; Obama was a political coward. The Benghazi event occurred during his 2012 campaign for president of the United States. Sacrificing those four American citizens was a more reasonable decision for him than to take any kind of action that would result in more American casualties. A major event would have been a campaign setback. He might have thought it would be politically safer just to 'let those four be sacrificed' for the sake of his political future. After all, "it was just a little bump in the road." A true military decision would have been to do whatever it takes to save American lives. He failed to do that. The next day - THE VERY NEXT DAY - he went on a fund-raising trip to Las Vegas.

Why didn't Hillary Clinton tell the whole truth about the Benghazi event? Because, that might be a negative mark against her if she plans to campaign for president in 2016. Apparently she thought it was safer just to shout, "What difference does it make how they died?"
Perhaps answers to what happened in "Fast and Furious" is just as important. We will consider that question next.

# 63

# Where are They?

The loss of high-powered weapons in 'Operation Fast and Furious' is another serious event that must have more answers; more honest answers. The Obama administration, including Barack Obama, personally, seems to have no interest in answering the cause of an innocent man's death. Obama will not let anyone in his administration even speak or whisper anything negative about any of his Muslim friends, yet he functions as if he cares nothing about an American citizen's life.

Where are those AK-47s? Why were they lost - unaccounted for, even though that was supposedly the purpose for the operation? Are they really lost, or are they hidden, waiting to be used against more innocent Americans when the right conditions arise for the Muslim Brotherhood to take some final action to 'destroy America' as they plan? I realize this question sounds absurd, but it's a question that should not be discounted until the administration gives a better answer.

Many reports say that radical Islamic terrorists are now training in certain parts of South America. What are their targets, what is their timing, and what weapons will they use?

# 64

# The Beast Rises

How and why will the Beast, the Antichrist, rise? It's most likely that a drive for personal power is the Beast's natural inclination. However, another possibility can't be totally discounted. Perhaps he could be following a plan by puppet-masters to create that 'New World Order.' We know what an autocratic government or a dictatorial government looks like. We've seen those come and go throughout history. The extremes go from much loss of life to total elimination of personal aspirations.

Ordinarily, over time, those collapse. But what might a New World Order look like? At the moment, that could consider three different scenarios. When either of these occur, it could represent the 'end of times' mentioned in the Bible.

The first could be a simple autocratic world government with a figurehead, or with a group acting as a figurehead. This is the organizational structure ordinarily envisioned when the concept of a one-world government is discussed. Under this form, countries would still exist as separate entities socially and religiously, but with all political decisions made by the central government. Likely, religious differences would be tolerated so long as nothing in that religion interfered with the concepts and dictates of the central government.

Of course, all military functions would be under the single authority and organization of the world leader. This would be to enforce dictates, and to prevent or discourage wars between assigned boundaries. Perhaps titles of those within assigned borders would be such as they were during the old Roman Empire; governor or proconsul.

Biblically, this could be the worst time for Israel. The leaders of Israel would have to make a serious decision; would they become a member of the new order? Or, would they have that option? According to Bible prophesy, this could be the time Israel is forced to agree to something they know might sign their death warrant. Perhaps Daniel 18: 23 and 25 gives a clue:

"And in the latter time of their kingdom, when the transgressors are come to full, a king of fierce countenance, and understanding dark sentences, shall stand up."

"And through his policy also he shall cause craft to prosper in his hand; and he shall magnify himself in his heart, and by peace shall destroy many -"

"And by peace shall destroy many." Perhaps that danger would begin slowly, such as signing a peace agreement to become a member of the world body to have access to world trade. Can you imagine a country completely cut off from imports or exports? Could a small country such as Israel provide itself with enough food, chemicals, mechanical devices and other raw materials to survive? They would have no choice if the world body made the decision to cut them off. Then, once Israel signs that agreement to become part of the world order and accepts the policies therein, what if the world order demands Israel give up its defensive weaponry?

# 65

# Obama's Satanic Ring

An article appeared on October 12, 2012, regarding Obama's ring. In that article it was stated that it's the same ring he has worn for many years and is also the ring used when Michelle Obama put it on his finger when they were married. That article suggested the ring had an engraving of part of the Shahada, the Islamic declaration that 'There is no god except Allah, and Mohammed is the messenger of Allah.'

Allegedly, according to that article, only the first half of the Shahada was engraved on the ring. The photograph of the ring had such low resolution it was not really clear what was engraved. Even experts asked to examine the photographs could not confirm that was the engraving. That allegation was later debunked when it was shown by photographs with better resolution cameras that the engraving was that of coiled serpents, not the Shahada.

That finding presented an even more disturbing scenario than what had been alleged. It made a direct connection to the 'seat of Satan' mentioned in Apostle John's writings to the seven biblical churches of Asia Minor, specifically the church at Pergamum, while he was exiled on the island of Patmos. John's indirect reference to the serpent opened  doors to discovering other connections between Satan and the serpent, often identified as the dragon or the beast in other areas of the Bible. The identifications of these names are often confusing. Generally, however, the serpent and the dragon, called in some places, 'that old dragon' refers to the devil. The serpent had his first introduction in the Garden of Eden. Obama proudly wears serpents on his ring.

References to the beast and the antichrist describe a different entity. And, the reference to the plural 'antichrists' is even different. There have been, and will be more antichrists. Only one antichrist is described throughout the Bible as the 'beast.' The other antichrists describe themselves, or are seen by others, as Jesus, the Messiah.

The most dangerous antichrist, the beast, will not assign himself to that role. Satan will choose him and assign him those great powers when Satan chooses. Now that person does not know he will become the End Times antichrist. This is according to Revelation, Chapter 13, the first two verses:

'And I stood upon the sand of the sea, and saw a beast rise up out of the sea, having seven heads and ten horns, and upon his horns ten crowns, and upon his heads the name of blasphemy. 2- And the beast which I saw was like unto a leopard, and his feet were as the feet of a bear, and his mouth as the mouth of a lion: and the dragon gave him his power, and his seat, and great authority.'

At this time, that person is building his power base thinking he's doing great things for mankind. He will get his full power, and that assignment to be that beast, that antichrist, when the seven continents, the seven heads, are combined under one rule."

# 66

# Supporting the Enemy

I finally decided there was no end to Obama's anti-American, anti-Christian actions and comments, so I decided to go ahead and close out the book. If he continues, I guess I will have to start another book. (I hope not - my golf game is really suffering. Of course my golf game has always suffered.)

Anyway, while I'm waiting for a proof copy of the book, I thought I should keep up my 'Crazy Conspiracy Theories' that many will assume is my purpose for writing these books and comments. I hope I'm not a 'crazy theorist.' In my 74-year-old mind, I'm a retired military officer who has served the country I love dearly. And, I have served in countries alien to American values and principles enough to recognize that difference. I see and feel that difference arising in our great nation. That's why I am so adamant, and determined to do 'my part.' That's why it's important that I express my concern about Obama courting and accepting the Muslim Brotherhood as strongly as he does.

Something has puzzled me greatly with Obama's election as president of the Untied States. Why did women and poor people vote for him overwhelmingly, when his actions are devastating them the most?

Obama's refusal to develop our own oil and gas resources is robbing scarce and important money from the pockets of poor people.

Rich people can afford to by gas. It's just an inconvenience for them to pay more. For poor people, it's devastating. They must have gas to get to work. Why would they vote for Obama to pay $5.00 a gallon, instead of $1.50 a gallon if we developed our own resources? There are many single young women head-of-households that are especially hurt by these prices. High gas prices result in higher-everything prices, especially food. And, people believe him when he blames 'greedy rich people' for their problems! If he had all the money from all the rich people, it wouldn't change a thing.

Instead of supporting America, Obama is supporting the Muslim Brotherhood. He buys oil from Saudi Arabia, and he's sending millions of dollars to other Muslim Brotherhood countries, especially Egypt. The Muslim Brotherhood has a written document stating they intend to 'Destroy the Western World - from within.' Should we not believe them? They are already on the way. What is the belief concept of the Muslim Brotherhood? It's called, 'Wahhabism.' The king of Saudi Arabia is the leader of that ideology.

Wahhabies as well as other Islamist fundamentalists believe in Sharia law. They extol the idea that it's the purest kind of law. Although they try to claim it's not extreme and against humanity, let's consider some of its rules, and what might happen to citizens of the United States if they were ever to rule here. To me, that doesn't seem farfetched from Obama's tendencies. There are 36 of these rules. Since this blog is getting rather long, I will list them in the next post. If you are interested, the information is from an article titled, 'Islamic Law in Brief!,' written February 4, 2011, by Syed Kamran Mirza.

# 67

# Islamic Sharia

Instead of supporting America, Obama is supporting the Muslim Brotherhood. He forces us to buy oil from Saudi Arabia, instead of allowing production of our own domestic oil reserves, and he's sending millions of dollars to other Muslim Brotherhood countries, especially Egypt. The Muslim Brotherhood has a written document stating they intend to 'Destroy the Western World - from within.' Should we not believe them? They are already on the way. What do they hope to force upon the entire world? Their Sharia law. What is Sharia law?

This is from an article titled, 'Islamic Law in Brief!,' written February 4, 2011, by Syed Kamran Mirza. He states, "These common laws of "Islamic Sharia" which are regularly practiced in the Islamically ruled (Sharia-based) nations with some minor variations:

1- Jihad defined as "to war against all non-Muslims to establish the religion" is the duty of every Muslim and Muslim head of state (Caliph). Muslim Caliphs who refuse jihad are in violation of Sharia and unfit to rule.

2- A Caliph can hold office through seizure of power, meaning through force.

3- The head of an Islamic State (Caliph) cannot be charged, let alone be punished for serious crimes such as murder, adultery, robbery, theft, drinking and in some cases of rape (Hudood cases) - Codified Islamic Law Vol 3 # 914C of and page 188 of Hedaya the Hanafi manual.

4- A percentage of Zakat (alms) must go towards jihad.

5- It is obligatory to obey the commands of the Caliph, even if he is unjust.

6- A Caliph must be a Muslim, a non-slave and a male.

7- The Muslim public must remove the Caliph in one case, if he rejects Islam.

8- A Muslim who leaves Islam (apostate) must be killed immediately.

9- A Muslim will be forgiven for murder of : a) an apostasy b) an adulterer c) a highway robber. Making vigilante street justice and honor killing acceptable.

10- A Muslim will not get the death penalty if he kills a non-Muslim.

11- Sharia never abolished slavery and sexual slavery and highly regulates it. A master will not be punished for killing his slave. Slavery still exists amongst Arab Muslims.

12- Sharia dictates death by stoning, beheading, for sins like killing, adultery, prostitutions; and other Quranic corporal punishments like: amputation of limbs (chopping hands and feet), floggings, beatings and other forms of cruel and unusual punishments even for the sins like: stealing, sexual promiscuity, robbery, burglary etc.

13- Non-Muslims are not equal to Muslims and must comply to Sharia (pay Zizzya: poll tax) if they are to remain safe. They are forbidden to marry Muslim women, publicly display wine or pork, recite their own religious scriptures, or openly celebrate their religious holidays or funerals. They are forbidden from building new churches or building them higher than mosques.

They may not enter a mosque without permission. A non-Muslim is no longer protected if he commits adultery with a Muslim woman or if he leads a Muslim away from Islam.

14- It is a crime for a non-Muslim to sell weapons to someone who will use them against Muslims. Non-Muslims cannot curse a Muslim, say anything derogatory about Allah, the Prophet, or Islam, or expose the weak points of Muslims. However, Muslims can curse, criticize or say anything derogatory they like to the religions of others.

15- A non-Muslim cannot inherit from a Muslim.

16- Banks must be Sharia compliant and interest is not allowed.

17- No testimony in court is acceptable from people of low-level jobs, such as street sweepers or a bathhouse attendant. Women in such low level jobs such as professional funeral mourners cannot keep custody of their children in case of divorce.

18- A non-Muslim cannot rule even over a non-Muslims minority.

19- Homosexuality is punishable by death.

20- There is no age limit for marriage of girls under Sharia. The marriage contract can take place anytime after birth and consummated at age 8 or 9.

Since this blog is getting a little long, the remaining law articles will be included in my next entry.

# 68

# More Sharia

What is the belief concept of the Muslim Brotherhood? It's called, 'Wahhabism.' The king of Saudi Arabia is the leader of that ideology. Wahhabism implies a strict form of Sharia law. I listed some of the articles of Sharia in my previous post. Following are the remaining articles from that post titled, 'Islamic Law in Brief,' by Syed Kamran Mirza:

21- Rebelliousness on the part of the wife nullifies the husband's obligation to support her, gives him permission to beat her and keep her from leaving the home.

22- Divorce is only in the hands of the husband and is as easy as saying: "I divorce you" and becomes effective even if the husband did not intend it.

23- There is no common property between husband and wife and the husband's property does not automatically go to the wife after his death.

24- A woman inherits half what a man inherits. Sister gets half of what brother gets.

25- A man has the right to have up to 4 wives and wife has no right to divorce him even if he is polygamous.

26- The dowry is given in exchange for the woman's sexual organs.

27- A man is allowed to have sex with slave women and also with women captured in battle (concubines), and if the enslaved woman is married her marriage is annulled.

28- The testimony of a woman in court is half the value of a man; that is, two women equal to one man.

29- A woman loses custody if she remarries.

30- A rapist may only be required to pay the bride-money (dowry) without marrying the rape victim.

31- A Muslim woman must cover every inch of her body which is considered "Awrah," a sexual organ. Some schools of Sharia allow the face and some don't.

32- A Muslim man is forgiven if he kills his wife caught in the act of adultery. However, the opposite is not true for women since he "could be married to the woman he was caught with."

33-It is obligatory for a Muslim to lie if the purpose is obligatory and is known as Taqiyya (Islamic Deception).

34. The perpetrators of genocide, mass rape and plunder will not be punished if they repent - Codified Islamic Law Vol 1 # 13.

35. To prove rape, a woman must have 4 male witnesses. Women's testimony is not accepted - Pakistan's Hudood ordnance 7 of 1979 amended by 8B of 1980. Thousands of raped women and girls in many countries have been charged with Zena (physical relations outside marriage) and punished by Sharia courts for want of witnesses.

36. All modern music including sexually explicit music of any kind is strictly prohibited and punishable by Islamic Sharia code of justice. Only Islamic songs are allowed.

So, with all these rules in Sharia Law, what does

Islam say about truth and honesty? It's required that Muslims defend Islam, even if they must be dishonest. In Mirza's article he emphasizes, "Caution! Islam permits devout Muslims to lie, cheat, and deliberately bluff non-Muslims to protect or promote his religion of Islam, anytime, anywhere. And this tactic is known as "Islamic Taqiyya" (Islamic deception), and was originally used by the Prophet of Islam to fool, and later subjugate and destroy enemies of Islam.

Is Barack Obama an expert is this 'Taqiyya?' He is sending millions (or billions) to the Islamists, and he's even including more of them in important positions in his administration. Yet, he claims America doesn't have enough money to provide escorts to give American children a tour of OUR White House!

And women voted overwhelmingly for Obama during the last election? What were they thinking!

# 69

# Irrational Treatment

This is an article copied from Brietbart that further discloses this plan by the Muslim Brotherhood - supported by Barack Obama - weakening the United States as we know it. This is also included in my up-coming book :

"In the Spring of this year, US Army Lieutenant Colonel Matthew Dooley was condemned by the Joints Chiefs of Staff (JCS) and relieved of teaching duties at Joint Forces Staff College for teaching a course judged to be offensive to Islam.

The course he taught, 'Perspectives on Islam and Islamic Radicalism', was an elective course that Lt. Col. Dooley's superiors judged as presenting Islam in a negative way. His superiors were persuaded to come to this conclusion after receiving an October 2011 letter in which 57 Muslim organizations claimed to be offended by the course.

The fact that Lt. Col. Dooley is a highly decorated combat veteran with nearly 20 years of service under his belt apparently held little or no sway with the JCS. As a matter of fact, JCS Chairman General Martin Dempsey personally attacked Lt. Col. Dooley on C-Span on May 10, 2012, during a Pentagon News Conference.

Yet the craziest part of all this is that "the course content, the guest speakers, and the method of instruction" for the course was all approved by the Joint Forces Staff College "years ago."

Former CIA agent Claire M. Lopez commented on the state of things: "All US military Combatant Commands, Services, the National Guard Bureau, and Joint Chiefs are under Dempsey's Muslim Brotherhood-dictated order to ensure that henceforth, no US military course will ever again teach truth about Islam that the jihadist enemy finds offensive (or just too informative)."

Of course this action against Lt. Col. Dooley is outrageous just on the face of it. But one must delve much deeper to understand the grave danger America now faces. The conspiracy is deep and multi-faceted, and is supported even by those who have taken an oath to 'protect and defend the United States against all enemies - foreign and domestic."

Of course, Obama's policies created this travesty

against Lt. Col. Dooley, but in my mind Obama's character is no better than that. That action can be expected by one of such little character. To me, the real travesty is from the actions by General Dempsey.

I spent over 20 years in the U.S. Air Force, serving a year of that in Saigon, Vietnam. At that time, and ever before and ever since, I have always had a high regard for military officers. They were expected, even of themselves, to be honest and honorable at all times, even under the most dire and self-incriminating situations.

To me, General Dempsey violated that military standard - that code. I realize he was following orders from either the secretary of defense or the president. I absolutely cannot believe he took that action against Lt. Col. Dooley of his own initiation and beliefs. Any honorable military officer would have resigned before committing that unwarranted assault against another military person - especially one of junior rank. That makes General Dempsey just as culpable in supporting the silent American jihad as the president. Who is General Dempsey, anyway. He is an unknown who came out of nowhere - selected, of course, by Barack Obama.

Perhaps that conclusion about Obama and his plans and actions for America must be made and accepted within each individual American heart. That thought is too dire - it's too unbelievable - to be expressed in written words in this insignificant and probably never-to-be-discovered book.

What are the real plans of this man, Barack Obama, who calls himself a Christian, but who too often supports the radical Islamist ideology? Who is this man who prepares for a personal political fund-raising trip to Las Vegas - while he knows four brave and patriotic American citizens are being slaughtered in Benghazi, Libya?

# 70

# His Snake

Whew! I finally got the first draft finished for the book, 'Obama's Ring: The Seat of Satan.' It should be available in less than a month. I didn't write it for profit, I wrote it for a message of awareness to the danger I believe Americans face. So, when it's finished, anyone who wants a free copy just send me an email address to attach and return, and I will reply with a free PDF copy - which can be sent as many times as you would like. If you don't respect Bible references then you definitely will not want to read the book.

I have already posted a copy of the front cover here on Authorsden. The serpent shown is a close-up copy of Obama's actual ring. It's taken from a photo of his ring at this site:

http://www.wnd.com/2012/10/obamas-ring-there-is-no-god-but-allah/

# 71

# Agenda 21

This is the direct copy of a headline on my AOL home page just a few minutes ago:

"The Obama administration said Tuesday the president has the authority to order deadly attacks on American citizens on US soil."

This is the quote that followed:

"The Obama administration believes it could technically use military force to kill an American on U.S. soil in an "extraordinary circumstance" but has "no intention of doing so," U.S. Attorney General Eric Holder said in a letter disclosed Tuesday."

The quote below is a paragraph I typed just today in my upcoming book. It describes a scene after people have been grouped in assigned communes to better utilize earth's resources. This fictitious president, Arabar, is discussing how to eliminate those who don't comply with the Agenda 21 applications:

"We already have enough control over the few

remaining military forces and some of our followers in the Homeland Security group, to take care of those scattered about in more isolated places." Arabar continued, "And, we have made great strides in our drone programs to eradicate those trouble-makers who will exist at the time of the great transition - and any who would attempt to isolate themselves after they have accepted the mark of the implanted chip. We already have small solar craft that can hover over an area for days watching for any suspected rebels. It's a simple matter of pushing a tiny button to fire the necessary shot from that drone."

Scary, isn't it what could happen? And, if it's conceivable even in fiction, it's possible to happen in real life. And, many people are calling me 'over the top?'

# 72

# Over the Top

I write letters to the editor almost monthly In my local area. And, I have been doing that for several years. Over that time, I've learned a few things about exposing your views in a public forum.

There was a time when public opinion exposure was fairly equally divided between left and right. Folks let their differences be known, but it was usually in a civil manner. I think that makes for a good public debate that's good for undecided American citizens, especially come voting time. A recent change has concerned me that the public discourse has become too one-sided. The right gets so harshly attacked that they choose not to face those attacks. I'm not.

After Obama began his campaign for 2008, the discourse became so harsh from the left that the public exchange in letters and blogs became an invitation to insult when one of the right submitted anything to be published. Letter writers and responders online to those letters became attacks instead of discourse.

It seems the writers from that opinion took a cue from what was happening from the Obama campaign strategy. That strategy was to 'attack the messenger' and disregard the message. As a result, for the last four years none of my comments have been rebutted on the face of the comments or message. But, I learn from every submission that I am the worst person on earth, I'm the most stupid person on earth who ever existed, and certainly a dire threat to humankind. And recently I learned that my ideas are 'over the top.' I guess I've been totally wrong about myself. I thought I was a pretty nice guy - at least that's what my wife of 53 years tells me.

Yes, I am very aware of my words and my actions, and the purpose for those words and ideas. Yes, I do walk a very thin line with my proposals, but I have never, never, never called anyone a name, other than their God-given name. I'm a very proud Republican who tries to set a standard of propriety. But, on the other hand, I will not stand idly by and watch my country be destroyed, as I see it, and say nothing. And, I would expect that from anyone else if they felt strongly enough that America was facing peril.

I feel America is facing a serious danger, and I will not stand idly by, and be blasted away because I'm afraid to be called a horrible name. I'm beginning to enjoy those recognitions. I'm learning many new names and adjectives I've never heard before.

My last four books, two fiction and two non-fiction, express my concern for this looming danger. The book I'm almost finished will be as strong as I can make it. It's titled, 'Obama's Ring: The Seat of Satan.' For those who forgot, this is in reference to the seat of Satan (serpents) in the Biblical church of Pergamum.

# 73

# Obama's Plan

In my upcoming book, I offer three possible reasons to explain why Barack Obama seems so determined to eventually become the one-world leader. If he's not trying to become the leader of something other than being the president of the United States, then why is he continuing to stay in his full campaign mode to destroy the Republicans? Why shouldn't he try to use his persuasive influence to cooperate and try to do what's best for America? He appears in full battle mode at all times to destroy his opposition and have his way.

He plans something greater for his future, possibly one of three options. The first option is to become the world leader described in the Bible Book of Revelation. The second option is to lead the Islamic world as their Mahdi to create their world of right and purity. The third possibility for his headstrong drive is to become the leader of the world under Agenda 21. Below is a partial explanation of that concept. It's explained further in the book - or it will be when it's completed.

Agenda 21 is a concept of establishing a one-world order to conserve natural resources and protect the planet. There are those among us who believe they can control our planet more effectively than God. They just discovered global warming and think they should be masters of it. God has warmed and cooled the planet for millions of years and He probably has a pretty good handle on things.

For example, a few thousand years ago the world was so cold that snow and ice permanently covered the United States almost to Texas. Then it slowly started warming and the ice line moved further northward. And, it's still moved closer to the Arctic Circle. It's happened before, then when God figured the time was right, He created another Ice Age. Sometimes He even flips things around and puts everything in different positions probably just to have a little fun. What was the seabed is now a high flat desert. What once was a mountain is now below the water.

I don't know if God does that just to have fun or for another reason; perhaps to keep the temperature on earth equalized over a long period of time; and perhaps also to counter the normal activity of erosion, that if left unchecked would make the earth totally flat and covered in water. Who knows why He does what He does, but I'm sure it's for a good reason. And, probably He does it much better than those who call themselves experts. Nevertheless, many seem to think they are smarter than God. So, they invented Agenda 21.

Al Gore, the man who discovered or invented global warming and the internet would be proud of ideas proposed in Agenda 21. Given enough time, I suspect years from now he will even be the one credited with inventing it, discovering it, or proposing it.

What is Agenda 21? Agenda 21 is a non-binding, voluntarily implemented action plan of the United Nations with regard to sustainable development. It's a product of the UN Conference on Environment and Development (UNCED) held in Rio de Janeiro, Brazil, in 1992. It's an action agenda for the UN, other multilateral organizations, and individual governments around the world that can be executed at local, national, and global levels. The '21' in Agenda 21 refers to the 21st century. It has been affirmed and modified at subsequent UN conferences. 'Agenda 21' is a 300-page document divided into 40 chapters that have been grouped into 4 sections.

# 74

# Skilled Manipulators

One chapter in my upcoming book contains a list of many people throughout history considered antichrists, according to the meaning in the Bible. The general definition is one who claims to be Christ, or who acts in the place of Christ, or who is considered to be Christ. One of our recent ones was Marshall Herff Applewhite, Jr. (May 17, 1931 - March 1997.) Remember him?
He's the one who led his people to plan for a space

flight to Heaven on a comet. Applewhite was an American religious leader who founded what became known as the Heaven's Gate religious group and organized their mass suicide in 1997. It was the largest mass suicide to occur inside the United States.

A native Texan, Applewhite attended several universities and then served in the U.S. Army. After finishing school he taught music at the University of Alabama. He later returned to Texas where he served in the music department at the University of St. Thomas, in Houston. He later met Bonnie Nettles, a nurse, and together they decided they were called to be divine messengers. In their early efforts they gained only one convert. He developed his new theology while serving in jail for not returning a rental car.

After his release he went to California and Oregon with Nettles. They eventually gained a group of followers. He initially stated that he and his followers would be visited by extraterrestrials that would give them new bodies with which they would ascend to a spaceship where their bodies would be transformed. He changed that ideology to say their bodies were merely containers of their souls which would be placed into new bodies. His partner, Nettles, died in 1985.

In the 1990s the group took more steps to publicize their theology. In 1996, they learned of the approach of Comet Hale-Bopp and rumors of an accompanying spaceship. They concluded that was the spaceship they were waiting for. They committed suicide in their mansion believing their souls would ascend to the spaceship where they would be given new bodies.

How could this happen? Some commentators attributed his followers' willingness to commit suicide to his skill as a manipulator. Others argued their willingness was due to their faith in the narrative he constructed. Others speculate that Applewhite had brainwashed his followers. This idea was rejected by many academics. Others suggest they followed him to suicide because they had become totally dependent on him and were poorly suited for life in his absence. Another said he accomplished that complete obedience of his followers by isolating them socially and cultivated an attitude of complete obedience to him. Most of the dead had been with him about 20 years. There were 21 women and 18 men who committed suicide with Applewhite.

Many citizens are beginning to see our president as one to worship. Many certainly see him as one who will save them. One group even proclaimed at their event, "Deliver us, Obama." More recently, Jamie Foxx also referred to Obama as a certain higher entity.

Is Obama one of those 'manipulators?' Where is he leading his many followers and worshipers?

# 75

# Islamic Struggle

The following comments are from an interview by Ryan Mauro, on RadicalIslam.org, with Salim Mansur, an associate professor teaching Political Science at the University of Western Ontario, London. Mansur is a Muslim:

Ryan Mauro:: Can you give us a brief overview of what the struggle within Islam is like right now, especially in North America?

Salim Mansur:

"The struggle within Islam in our time is between
Muslims who embrace the values of the modern world in
terms of freedom, individual rights, gender equality and
democracy on the one side and Muslims who oppose
these values and, hence, modernity on the basis of
Sharia.

This struggle, therefore, goes to the very heart of how
Muslims understand Islam either as a faith-tradition, or
as a total system of belief and practice that is antithetical
to the norms of the modern world. In other words, for
Muslims who embrace modernity, as I do, Islam is a
matter of personal belief and not a political system; and
Muslims opposed to modernity view Islam ideologically,
hence Islamism, and accordingly they embrace the views
of Maudoodi and Hasan al-Banna, Syed Qutb and
Khomeini, about Islam as a totalitarian value-system.

The seeds of this struggle or, more appropriately, the
basis of conceiving Islam ideologically and in terms of
politics and power might be traced back to the earliest
years of Islam and Muslim history. But it is in our time,
beginning in the middle years of the last century,
Muslims have had to face the challenge of modernity
when Muslim societies became independent states
following the end of colonial rule by European powers.

This is a complex story. Let me note here only the
following. The Muslim states sociologically speaking are
almost without exception mostly poor developing
countries wherein is found just about every aspect of
under-development.

Despite the few states of the Middle East possessing
petro-wealth, Muslim societies are relatively backward
culturally, politically, technologically, and Muslims, in

general, are denied freedom by those in power and who use Islam as an ideological instrument in legitimating their authority. (The next paragraph says a lot.) It is only in the midst of freedom and democracy found in North America that anti-Islamist Muslims can make their case, give moral support to anti-Islamists in the Muslim world, expose the nature of politics that make for such deplorable and, ultimately, evil alliance as that between the United States and Saudi Arabia, and question the West's support for governments in the Muslim world that are more or less opposed to the values of freedom, individual rights, women's equality, equal rights for and protection of minorities, and the norms of democracy.

But the lack of support for anti-Islamist Muslims in the media, and by government and non-government agencies, has meant in a cruel twist of politics that the most virulently anti-Western Muslims, the Islamists, are mostly listened to and their views receive undue attention in the making of public policy in respect to the Muslim world or individual Muslim states, in reporting news about the Muslim world, and in the prevalent dominant narrative about Islam.

Hence, the irony that North American institutions, government and non-government, instead of assuming the positive role of assisting in some measure the reform of Islam through support for anti-Islamist Muslims have done just the opposite, and frequently, by amplifying the voices of Islamists in the free world."

# 76

# Obama Blasphemy

I can't get to the end to close it out. Obama keeps doing things, every day, that add to my upcoming book. What will he do or say today that will add more emphasis to describe his contempt for America? I planned a 100-page book. I'm already up to 255 pages. This is an excerpt of an addition I had to add about his speech on March 21: (Referencing the book, 'King Obama: America's Greatest Danger.')

"For the moment let's just ask the question; who would bow in the presence of a Muslim leader - other than a Muslim? Certainly it must be someone who felt inferior to that person. Did Obama feel inferior because of world position, time in position, or because Obama himself is a Muslim of lower rank than the Saudi king? There was a reason. Obama never explained that reason. Apparently, he feels his worshipers love him so much he does not need to express a reason. They will just follow him over the cliff with their eyes closed - without questioning. In any case, his bow in subservience demonstrated disrespect to the status of the United States of America, and more importantly - blasphemy against God.

Two incidents mentioned earlier will be repeated here. They're so significant, for this discussion, they deserve a double-take:

Would a Christian routinely blaspheme God, as Barack Obama continues to do? Other than those incidents already mentioned, another more blatant blasphemy occurred on April 16, 2009 by the Obama group.

On that date, Obama required the monogram, consisting of the letters IHS, for the name of Jesus, be covered before he made his speech at Georgetown University. The monogram above an archway was covered with black painted plywood. Certainly he would not consider this blasphemy - black painted plywood covering the symbol of Jesus. Yet, on March 21, 2013, he proudly stood under a large background picture of Yasser Arafat - the 'Father of Islamic terrorism' - as he gave his speech to the Palestinians in Ramallah. Does that not boldly suggest his inclinations?

Obama was also recorded at a closed-door fundraiser in San Francisco making disparaging comments about religion. He said, "You go into these small towns in Pennsylvania and, like a lot of small towns in the Midwest, it's not surprising they get bitter, they cling to guns and religion or antipathy to people who aren't like them or anti-immigrant sentiment or anti-trade sentiment as a way to explain their frustrations."

His comment didn't specifically say 'Christians' but that's the dominant religion referred to in the Midwest. A reference that clinging to religion (Christianity) out of bitterness and frustration and not out of search for truth and salvation is another bold example of his common blasphemy against Christ and the Bible. So, which religion or group does Obama really support? Research many of his close contacts and you will discover many more.

# 77

# King Obama

My new book: 'King Obama: America's Greatest Danger,' is now available in Kindle. There's a little problem with the formatting - the contents page didn't format correctly, but the text pages are correct. I'm leaving it available on Kindle until the paperback version is approved. That should be tomorrow. Then I will change the Kindle format which will be another day.

The book has 316 pages with 13 chapters and some extra items at the end. The 13 chapters are titled: 1 - Hoping for the Savior. 2 - Obama's Hatred of America. 3 - Rise of Big Brother. 4 - Deceit is Honesty. 5 - Cooperating With Terrorists. 6 - Deadly Secrets. 7 - Dangerous Deceptions. 8 - A Police State. 9 - A New America. 10 - Obama's Foundation. 11 - The King Rises. 12 - Rise of Islam. 13 - The Antichrist.

The end matter includes: 'Things Never to Forget' (Such as Benghazi and Fast and Furious) 'Four Famous Quotes,' and 'Saul Alinsky's 12 Rules of Confrontation.'

# 78

# Rule 5

Why is Barack Obama calling the recent scandals against his administration - "Phony Scandals?" Obviously, he's referring to the IRS scandal, the AP scandal, Fast and Furious, and the Benghazi event - unless there are other scandals that we don't know about. People died in Fast and Furious - and in the Benghazi event. Why would Obama say something this infuriating to those concerned?

The answer: It's from RULE 5 of the Saul Alinsky guide book, which says, "Ridicule is man's most potent weapon." There is no defense. It's irrational. It's infuriating. It also works as a key pressure point to force the enemy into concessions. The purpose is to create anger and fear. In effect, Obama is trying to distract from the important questions of the scandals by distracting with the reaction to his absurd comments. He wants to create the 'anger' response.

But, what does Obama know about Saul Alinsky? This extract from my upcoming book, 'King Obama' explains in part:

"More information about Obama, Gamaliel, and Saul Alinsky continues, from Theobamafile.com in an article titled, The Gamaliel foundation - Obama Meets Alinsky:

Obama first learned Alinsky's rules in the 1980s, when Alinskyite radicals with the Chicago-based Alinsky group Gamaliel Foundation recruited, hired, trained and paid him as a community organizer in South Side Chicago. They also helped him get into Harvard Law School to "learn power's currency in all its intricacy and detail," as Obama put it in his memoir. A Gamaliel board member even wrote a letter of recommendation for him.

Obama took a break from his Harvard studies to travel to Los Angeles for eight days of intense training at Alinsky's Industrial Areas Foundation, a station of the cross for acolytes. In turn, he trained other community organizers in Alinsky agitation tactics. In 1988, he even wrote a chapter for the book: 'After Alinsky: Community Organizing in Illinois,' in which he lamented organizers' "lack of power" in implementing change.

What is the Gamaliel and the Barack Obama connection?"

My upcoming book explores Obama's association with the Gamaliel organization in great detail. It also uncovers many other connections he had with other extreme organizations and people.

# 79

# How Could it Happen?

Have you ever wondered if or how America could be taken over by foreign invaders, or others in our country who would disregard our Constitution and the freedom it's designed to protect? My new political thriller: America 20XX: The New World Order, describes exactly how that could happen.

This 100,000 word story describes our vulnerability from an economic crisis created by oil prices controlled by foreign governments. That lack of funding causes local police and security agencies to be weakened, and replaced by a federal constabulary. That security force is named Vision. A foreign king conspires with the American president to use Vision as the Islamic jihad to conquer The United States. This story is inspired by current conspiracy theories. Although fictional, many character names might be associated with real people by those with conspiracy imaginations.

Fictionally, the story gives explanations and conspiracy definitions of many current terms and social conditions. For example: political correctness is a weapon used by two conspiracy plans to destroy American's resolve and willingness to fight against the invaders. Many of these invaders are flowing in through our open borders. The intentional destruction of America's education effectiveness is necessary to weaken young citizens' understanding and respect for our United States Constitution and our national identity.

Can America be saved from these insidious traitors and attackers? Of course, but the real mystery in this action novel is - how?

# 80

# A Fictional Account

America 20XX: The New World Order, my new political thriller, is now available at links through AuthorsDen. In this novel, the fictional characters explain many of our current world political problems and how they are synchronized to destroy American liberty and freedom. These characters also try their hardest to keep these disasters from becoming institutionalized into our society.

Fictionally, of course, this novel explains why gas prices are so high, and why they will keep rising. Also, fictionally, it explains why food prices will continue to escalate, and why food quality will deteriorate, and much will rot in the dirt in which it is grown. These two price rises are connected to the coming Islamic jihad. This novel also explains, fictionally of course, why many Christian churches and Jewish synagogues will be destroyed. And, it demonstrates how easy it would be, with surreptitious support from a rogue president, for Islamic jihadists to be welcomed by many deceived American citizens, as they march past their Conquest Mosque in New York City.

Presently, there are two conspiracy theories that propose threats to American freedom. One is the radical Islamic encroachment. The other is the Socialist/Marxist/Progressive movement. These two are not compatible. Terrorism demonstrates the extreme form of anarchy, while socialism demonstrates an extreme form of governmental control. This novel, fictitiously of course, explains what happens when these two factions face each other in their determination to destroy American Constitutional freedoms.

'When all is said and done,' (a great ABBA song) can four old, has-been, retired military people: Carl, Richard, Bob, and Marty, stop this threat to America that perhaps has already gone too far to turn back? With the help of Texas Governor John Marker and Arizona Governor, Ann Melody, we certainly hope so. God bless America.

This book: America 20XX: The New World Order, is now available at Amazon and Barnes and Noble. It's also available in Kindle and other digital download formats at Amazon.

# 81

# Internal Security

My political thriller, America 20XX: The New World Order, gives a fictional account of negative events now happening to us in America. It gives a coordinated look at current questions that affect the everyday lives of Americans. For example, is the drastic and continued rise in gas prices a deliberate conspiracy to create frustration and weakness that will invite Islamic jihadists to invade America? Is the government's refusal to control our borders associated with that conspiracy? Is a president's refusal to allow a positive energy policy part of that danger? Is an effort to ban ownership of private weapons another important part of that <u>fictional</u> conspiracy?

I started this novel a year ago when I saw dangerous and callous events taking place that clearly threaten the survival of this great democracy our forefathers fought to give us. First, our government refuses to allow use of our expansive natural resources: oil, gas, and coal. That means we must send more money to those oil producing countries that hate us - so they can keep funding terrorists who plan to destroy our strength and resolve. They must do that before they can totally annihilate Israel, without risk.

Secondly, too much of our corn crops are being used for ethanol. This is not for a substitute energy purpose, it's for a subsidy purpose to buy more votes and support from those wealthy and influential farmers growing corn. It has no energy value. It will only create a food shortage which will create despair for many, and devastation for the poor. But, is that what our leaders want so they can take more direct control over our everyday lives? If many states go bankrupt, what happens? Can states afford to provide security in a chaotic and bankrupt environment?

Third, when that chaos erupts who will provide security? Will it be a new federal constabulary? If we no longer have the right to own defensive weapons, will our freedom be vulnerable to that federal police force, especially if that force is comprised of people who do not share the same American principles of freedom and democracy as we do? Perhaps these actions, taking place as we watch without recourse, are the greatest threat to Americans since the Revolutionary War. For our survival, we must never give up our right to own firearms. There will be a new attack on that right coming soon!

To make this book available to more concerned citizens, I have just reduced the price on Kindle from 9.95 to 3.95. It's as low as I can make it. Also, you don't have to have a Kindle book to read this on your computer. There is a free Kindle application download at Amazon for PCs.

# 82

# A Raptor?

Have you ever heard of an aircraft in the U.S. arsenal called the F-22 Raptor? It's the most advanced fighter aircraft ever created. It's so sophisticated, stealthy, and effective that after building less than 200, our government and military strategic planners decided to eliminate funding for more because it's too advanced for current modern use.

Guess what? During Defense Secretary Gate's visit to China, he was introduced to a new Chinese version of the same aircraft. They are now beginning to produce them. I wonder why. What are their plans? Have we chosen to voluntarily make our country vulnerable to threats and coercion? I ask this question because the F-22 Raptor was an integral part of defending America against invading Islamic jihadists in one of my books. It might also be needed against others who would threaten our security. These aircraft were necessary to help save America in my novel. Will they be necessary to defend the United States in the future? Have our leaders made a severe strategic blunder? Why?

# 83

# Ban Weapons?

How quickly history is forgotten. While the debate about private gun ownership will go on, probably forever - as it should since it's a serious question, private ownership plays an important role in protecting a country from invasion, both foreign and domestic. Most, except those of us in the 'older generation' do not know that America and its allies were reluctant to invade mainland Japan near the end of World War II because all Japanese citizens, not just the military, were prepared to attack anyone who came onto their shores. Had it not been for the big bomb, today's free world as we know it might not exist.

That brings to question: what if our shores - or southern borders - were attacked while our military was fully engaged elsewhere around the world? Would those Second Amendment haters then say, "Boy, I sure wish we had some guns, and knew how to use them!"

What if, as has already been proposed, the federal government were to develop a federal civil police force. And, what if that federal constabulary did not function under Constitutional principles. Would those Second Amendment haters begin to wonder why that Constitutional right is so important?

My writing about the 'New World Order' is the

strongest statement I could make supporting private ownership of private weapons. It's a story about an Islamic jihad, supported by a treasonous government. The first act by the fictitious jihadists - and the government - is to ban and confiscate all private weapons. Those who refuse to comply are shot! The question is: what happens if you can't protect yourself, your family, or our country?

# 84

# Two Countries in One

Okay, I just made another check mark in my novel regarding how world events are making America more vulnerable to the coming Islamic jihad. Yesterday, I put the check mark on the chapter concerning intentional degradation of our education system to accept radical Islam. Today, my check mark is on Europe's concern about multi-culturalism.

Within the last week, many European leaders have expressed their concern about Islamists separating themselves within their new countries; especially England, Germany and France. Not only are they separating themselves, they are forcing their adopted countries to allow them to be a country within a country. Now we see that same thing beginning to happen in the United States. And, is anyone in Obama's administration, including Barack Obama, trying to discourage their plan to form their own government's within our country? If so, they are keeping it a secret among themselves.

# 85

# Food Anarchy

Could a food shortage, or high prices, create a major hardship for American citizens in the near future? Throughout history, food has played an important role in world events, and in the health and prosperity of individual countries. Even one of our important Biblical stories is based on a seven-year drought in Egypt. According to current news reports, food prices was a major reason for unrest now taking place, again, in Egypt. And, we shouldn't forget the many African nations, where starvation is routine and anarchy commonplace.

This could this happen in America; and from two reasons. First, oil prices could become so high that transportation of food would be too expensive to move from state to state. Second, too much arable land could be converted to production of ethanol that a minor drought would create an agricultural disaster. Could that drought last seven years like in Egypt?

How could this happen? One of my novels, fictionally of course, suggests a treasonous president might make it happen on purpose, to support a well-planned Islamic jihad to invade America. That president refuses to allow energy production, other than a full focus on ethanol. The new federal constabulary, secret jihadists, is welcomed by states to quell the rising unrest.

The underlying purpose for this novel is to stress the importance of having a sound and clear energy policy, which we do not have. Government refuses to accept this urgent and important responsibility to preserve our freedom. Why?

# 86

# Planned Failure

Although we keep bemoaning the problems with our education system, there is no serious plan to fix it. Those at the highest level who control education policies will not allow it to be improved; within the context of what patriotic Americans consider 'improved.'

Clearly, 'improvement' in the context of our federal government is that which is in compliance with the coming new world order; which means compliant and controllable, not educated. The move by the U.S. Department of Education to institute Islamic culture into American schools, as demonstrated recently in Texas, more blatantly exposes their underlying scheme. They care not about our students and our prosperity; they care only about how they are perceived as a respected partner in the new world order. The further the U.S. Department of Education guides our children away from literacy and comprehension, the closer we become to fulfilling their objective.

With caring and supportive parents, this threat could be defeated, but we are beyond that point already. Too many parents are unprepared to guide their children's education needs. Furthermore, the government promotes the idea that only more money and better teachers are needed. They have alienated marginal parents from that parental responsibility, which began with James Coleman's concept of 'social capital' education, in 1966.

The greatest threat to our children's education is the U.S. Department of Education. It must be obliterated, wiped from the face of the earth, and remembered only as a dangerous nightmare.

# 87

# Money and Education

Many recent letters have made heart-wrenching and psychological pleas that more money is needed to make education more effective. These pleas have only an emotional basis, and offer no proof that more money results in better education. Close evaluation of the Mississippi Report Card since the first one in 1994 reveals standard results regardless of funding.

Consistently, money shows no correlation to education results. The graduation rate in 1994 was approximately 61 percent, and it's still the same today.

The only standard correlation to education results is the poverty level. Ten states with the highest poverty level have a 62 percent graduation rate. Ten states with the lowest poverty level have an 85 percent graduation rate. Poverty involves family conditions which ordinarily reflects a weak education culture. Many children believe they are failures before they enter the third grade. Our education system supports that belief and offers shock instead of motivation. How can students motivate themselves when told there's not enough money to give them a real education?

How can we help these weak students motivate themselves and find the real personal value of learning? I say, "Down with compound fractional equations and all their worthless friends such as the Pythagorean theorem, sines and cosines." I have never seen one of these useless animals outside an education environment. First, teach students functional disciplines of which they can understand and respect the value. The first principle of motivation is to understand 'why.' With deeper understanding comes more acceptance of the broader disciplines.

The Obama administration has reversed the purpose for education. Now, it's to teach children how to become dependent upon society, how to become more multi-cultural and anti-American, and how to learn more about Allah and the Koran. He still asks for more money for education, especially Pre-K. Money is not, nor has it ever been the answer to better education. It starts within the family and the cultural environment - of expectations.

# 88

# What's Important?

Why are our students not learning enough in many of our schools to be more literate? I blame it on those darn compound fractional equations. I remember having to study those obnoxious animals when I was in school, over fifty years ago. I thought their importance was way overblown at that time, 1952, and I tried to ignore them. I guess enough of them hid in my hair so they could expose themselves during test time. I don't remember if I passed that test or simply ignored it.

They escaped from my life for forty years. If I had seen one during that time, I probably would have thought it was only a regular algebra thing trying to sexually expose itself. Anyway forty years later, that compound fractional equation (CFE) thing arose from the ashes and poked its tongue out at me again. I taught an algebra class for a GED student, who lacked only algebra to get her high school diploma. They raised their ugly faces again during that class and we went to the mat in a tug of war again. Maybe I won that match because that young lady passed the GED test. I thought those CFEs had finally disappeared from the face of the earth, where they belonged. But, was I fooled - they raised their ugly faces again.

# King Obama Blogs

Ten years ago, I decided to do my civic duty and be a substitute teacher at a local school. The call came at 6:30 one morning, and I had to be at the class at 7:30 - that same morning. Dutifully, I showed up on time, and was told I would be teaching a 6<sup>th</sup> grade math class, and that the teacher had left the lesson plans on her desk. Since she had scheduled her time off month's ago, I had a logical question: why wasn't I called the day before, so I could plan for the day - and understand the lesson plan. She was to be gone for two months. The school policy was not to call a substitute until the day needed. Wow! Anyway, guess what the lesson plan was for that day? Okay, don't guess - we all know. That teacher was very smart and sneaky. She got out of town rather than face those dreaded CFEs.

After those 6<sup>th</sup> graders decided they couldn't intimidate a mature man (okay, an old man) they got serious about pretending to realize CFEs were important. I also pretended they were important, and would be a major consideration in their success or failure in life. The one boy who was most obnoxious suddenly became my best buddy when I showed him step-by-step how easy it was to stare down those obnoxious CFEs.

The purpose for this story, which is true, is that many children who could be successful, happy, and productive, are driven from a real education and positive dreams by having to face compound fractional equations. Becoming literate with functional disciplines is far more important than compound fractional equations. I have never seen one outside a classroom, and I doubt if the reader of this post has ever seen one outside a classroom. Who needs one? Then, along came the Pythagorean theorem.

# 89

# Our Constitution

According to our U.S. Constitution: "No person except a natural born citizen, or a citizen of the United States, at the time of the adoption of the Constitution, shall be eligible to the office of President." (Article 2, Section 1)

Freedom is a precious, and possibly fleeting thing. It can be lost in a still moment if its protectors are not vigilant. Few people in the world, since its existence, have had the freedoms given to U.S. citizens under our Constitution. Occasionally, in our past, actions by our government have strayed from the letter and intent of that guiding document. However, that movement has not been too far away from the document's purpose: to protect freedom and liberty. When actions have strayed too far, it has always been jerked back to compliance by watchful and concerned patriots.

However, could total disregard and abandonment of our guiding American principles begin with a single minor omission to comply with our Constitution, or an overlooked falsehood? If we respect our Constitution, and believe in its principles, should we not respect all of it, unless and until a majority of citizens rightfully amend that part which might be offensive to our freedoms?

Another important question is: what is the underlying

intent of someone who would be president of the United States knowing he or she is not eligible? Is that not, in itself, a blatant disregard to our Constitution? If that action is a falsehood, how can the intent of further action be trusted?

Most requirements of our Constitution have laws to enforce them. This Article is only a statement without an enforcement mechanism. Would it not be appropriate for state attorneys general to require a valid birth certificate be filed with the state before one's name may be added to the state's ballot? Is asking one responsible for protecting our Constitution to comply with that Constitution asking too much?

# 90

# Improving Education

Who and what is our greatest education failure? In some states the dropout rate is more than 60 percent. In many local communities, the dropout and failure rate is even higher than that. Are we failing our children, or are our children failing society?

Students drop out, while many teachers march in picket lines and protest for their own personal status. Students hear from responsible educators that they can't be educated (they can't get smart) unless society gives more money to teachers and the concept of education.

How should students interpret these actions of teachers, many of whom they love and respect?

Most teachers probably love to teach and are personally concerned about the future of their students. However, so much publicity about education concerns money that students certainly must be adversely affected. Are too many being brainwashed that they can't learn because education doesn't have enough money to give them an effective education? Why stay in school and try to learn if society has already determined they can't learn?

How can education effectiveness really be improved? How can we give each child a valid opportunity to learn and be successful within his or her dreams and aspirations? The answer is too simple for education policy-makers to even consider. They must keep the system complicated to justify their high positions. The answer is known as the 'problem-solving process.'

First, the highest education policy-makers must determine, and broadcast on every street sign, the primary purpose for education. That was done before 1975, when the U.S. Department of Education was established. To make the system work again, that department must be abolished, eliminated, and wiped from the face of the earth.

Then, education must be recognized by its three parts. It's not just 'education.' It's opportunity, motivation, and supportive conditions. Society provides opportunity. Family and culture provides conditions. Each student must have a reason to be motivated. One of those reasons is a clear purpose. Society has failed miserably instilling that purpose.

# 91

# Paying More

Socialism - only a step away. How has President Obama been so successful in leading America further and deeper into Socialism? Class warfare has been his greatest open and public tool. His words suggest that since some people are successful, they have prevented others like most of us from being that successful. He masterfully uses envy as a tool to turn middle class and lower class citizens against those who have more. He manipulates that envy to gain votes, believing his followers will support him to make those "evil successful people" pay their fair share. If that's not his plan, why does he keep casting such big stones at the more successful people?

During his railing speeches, he fails to say that almost half our American citizens pay no income tax: nada, zero, nothing. Many of those even get money back when they file, in the form of earned income credits. Successful citizens already pay most of the income tax.

What is Obama talking about? And, how much is their fair share? All their income? He has never said what that fair share should be: fifty-percent, sixty-percent, ninety percent? Any person who understands logic and brainwashing can see his tactic is an emotional appeal.

It's not factual reality. Who can and should say what that fair share should be - when they pay most of the income taxes already?

Now for the biggest joke of all. I heard him say today that the most successful should pay more of their fair share to help pay down the national debt. What's the joke? If Obama has more money in the treasury, it would not go to pay down the national debt. It would be spent to buy more votes for Obama. When has he shown any concern for our national debt - that our children, grandchildren, great-grand-children and beyond will be paying?

How does this evolve into his plan for Socialism? If he is re-elected, our national debt will continue to grow and will accelerate. At some point there will be riots and protests. The only way to explain a way out of the problem is to nationalize all industries so they can be programmed and controlled by the government, for more efficiency and output to create more profit to repay all that debt. At that time Obama will have bought enough votes and have enough supporters that his transition to Socialism will be supported by most of those citizens.

This Pied Piper knows exactly what he is doing. Do those who follow him, without question, have their eyes open?

# 92

# The Big Stick

During his speech on April 26, Joe Biden announced, 'President Obama has a big stick. I promise you, he has a very big stick.' In a much earlier speech, Obama said the United States needs a domestic civil police force equally as powerful as our military. Combining these two comments should cause American citizens great concern.

Our Founding Fathers warned us of the danger of a national police force. We have never had one. A national police force could invite a national leader 'with a big stick' to proclaim himself 'President for life,' 'King of America,' or the 'Great Imam' and no one could challenge him - not even our military. Just recently, General Patraeus, an honorable patriot, was removed from a high military position that could have been considered a threat to Obama's agenda. At the moment, no one knows the name of any senior military leader. They have been obscured and pushed way into the background.

Even now, our national leaders are afraid to challenge Obama's self-appointed authority. Why aren't our influential congressmen and senators challenging his arbitrary unconstitutional actions. He has placed czars in powerful positions to control every aspect of our lives while congress stands back with their eyes closed. He also promotes Muslim encroachment of our country while ignoring reasonable ideas from other religions, especially Christians. He allows bullies to stand at voting places, unchallenged, to intimidate citizen voters. Perhaps he has already decided voting will become an obsolete activity.

What 'big stick' did he use against Mayor Cory Booker to make him  recant statements against his political strategy? Is his big stick made up of promises or of serious threats? I think that answer becomes more obvious in the tone of his voice as he makes more of those promises.

More recently, Senator Dianne Feinstein was forced to an immediate about-face when she said something not supporting Obama's agenda. What did he promise her to change her comments, or was it more of a threat than a promise? In her position, she has nothing to gain by a 'promise.' What was the threat - that big stick? How soon will he use it against ordinary citizens?

# 93

# Too Many Czars

How is it possible that so many regulations and rules are strangling America's ability to create new businesses and more jobs, thereby weakening America's ability to defend itself and maintain our traditional American economic, social, moral and religious culture? While the president is out front reading dynamic and accusatory speeches from his telepromptor, his appointed minions and hatchet-men are skulking in the background grinding America to a halt. Now, one has to apply for a permit to apply for a permit to create a new business. The rules they produce are to restrict anything productive. Just consider Boeing's effort to create new jobs in South Carolina. And consider our energy policy.

How is he doing this? By appointments to high administration positions without confirmation by the U.S. Senate. Consider: H.W. Bush had 3 appointees, 2 classified as czars, all confirmed by the Senate. Clinton had 11 appointees, 8 classified as czars, 7 not confirmed by the Senate. G.W. Bush had 49 appointees, 33 classified as czars, 28 not firmed by the Senate. Obama has 42 appointees, 38 classified as czars, and 33 not confirmed by the Senate.

If the normal confirmation process, established by our Constitution, continues to be ignored and trampled upon are we not giving our country away to despots and those who seek concentrated and centralized power? That presents an even more dangerous question to our democratic survival. If a president decided to appoint himself as President for Life, who could stop him if all the other branches of government are inactive and neutralized? One might say, "Our military would never allow that." But, what if our military was also confused and neutralized by a powerful czar? Two of his czars have already been exposed as communist-socialists and forced to resign - only by publicity - not by administration choice.

# 94

# Martyr Book

Call it interesting; call it a coincidence; call it random chance. In 2010, I drove from Mississippi to California. Along the way - and it was a long way to drive - we passed by a town in Arizona called, Casa Grande. It's at the intersection of Interstates 8 and 10, between Tucson and Phoenix. As I drove past Casa Grande on I-8 to the bypass to I-10, the area to the south looked really barren. I said to my wife, "Wouldn't this be a great location for Islamic jihadists to infiltrate into the United States?"

That impressed me so much that when I returned home, I wrote a book about jihadists infiltrating across the border at Casa Grande, aided by Mexican drug smugglers. I released the book on Amazon on January 15, 2011. On January 27, 2011, Border Patrol agents reported they had just found an Iranian jihadist book titled, 'In Memory of our Martyrs,' in the desert near Casa Grande. To say the least, that was a bit scary. You can google that book for more information - really.

That was the same time the Arizona governor was trying to stop the illegal immigration flow from the south, and the Obama administration was determined to keep her administration from protecting the borders. As I think about that Arizona border now, I wonder who the greatest threat to our national security might be?

I sent copies of my book, 'America 20XX: The New World Order,' to libraries in the area around Casa Grande. Anyone living in that area should be able to read it through those libraries. God bless America - and Governor Brewer.

# 95

# Jihadists

In the Republican debate last night, Rick Santorum mentioned there was suspicion or evidence that Iranian terrorists were being trained in South America, especially in Venezuela. They plan to infiltrate into the United States through the Mexican border, assisted and led by drug lords. It's suspected that's the reason the president of Iran and his emissaries have been visiting Hugo Chavez so often.

Very interesting. My book, America 20XX: The New World Order, written over a year ago, has that very scenario. It tells how they will infiltrate, where they will strike first, and details how the U.S. president - of course, fictional in the story - helps them succeed in their initial attacks. The story also details how and why the terrorists and drug dealers work together, and why and how the terrorists are accepted into American society to remain underground until they are called to action.

# 96

# The Last Election

I was only six years old when President Franklin Roosevelt died, but I remember the public fear that no one could take his place. When Harry Truman was sworn into office on April 12, 1945, everyone believed all was lost in the world: the Germans would win, and Japan would rule the Pacific and invade America. How did I know this you ask? We didn't have television in those days, only a radio that required a long antenna if you were within range of a station. Our television was the weekly 'Newsreel' when we went to the movies. Boy were they fast-paced and exciting.

Anyway, although everyone considered that clothing store owner from Missouri, Harry Truman inept and incapable, the Germans were defeated a month later. The Japanese surrendered in August, 1945 after Truman gave the order to drop two atomic bombs on Hiroshima and Nagasaki. I felt part of that win, because my mother was a welder at Ingalls Shipyard in Pascagoula, MS, from 1942 till 1944. Although too young to know what was happening, I nevertheless knew everyday life was uncertain and stressful. We survived, and we are free Americans today because no leader is irreplaceable.

It was there, in Pascagoula, in 1943, that I first heard

Gene Autry sing 'Rudolph the Red-Nosed Reindeer.' That was from a jukebox in a restaurant on the corner of Mantou St. and Ingalls Blvd. I was four years old. I still remember Mantou St., because then, to me, it sounded like 'man toe.'

At that time, America thought Roosevelt was irreplaceable. He had served three terms, and was three months into his fourth term when he died. That's right - he served as president over twelve years. Harry Truman proved that no one is irreplaceable. Soon after, in 1951, we saw the $22^{nd}$ Amendment passed that limited the president to two four-year elected terms, and ten-years total.

Why is this information important? What would happen if a power-hungry president did not want to give up that power at the end of a second term, especially if that president had total disdain for our U.S. Constitution, as does our current president? He has already said the Constitution gets in the way of things he wants to accomplish to make the country better. If a national leader doesn't have total respect for our constitution, how can he be expected to lead us to that destiny foreseen by our Founding Fathers? And, as with a national crisis - world crisis - facing America in the 1930s-1940s, could not a leader who imagined himself the supreme being hesitate to take total control of a nation today, especially if he were part of creating that crisis for that ulterior purpose? A decision regarding Iran could create that perfect scenario.

What might happen if we have a severe world crisis in the next few years? Would our president comply with our Constitution and allow transition to another duly elected person? Or would he proclaim the situation too great to allow a transition?

# 97

# A Deciding Point

In this year, 2012, Americans will experience another important decision, an event that will determine the character of our country and our personal freedoms for the next generation, and perhaps beyond. This election year likely will determine whether America remains united, or becomes many Americas separated by culture, class, economic status, and religious dogmas alien to those that have long guided the positive character of our great country. After 2012, will we have the opportunity to make a choice?

In his voracious zeal for personal power, one man promises more free things to the growing masses, their fair share, in return for their votes to keep him in power to give more free things to those who wait with their hands out for those free things. He apologizes for America's character and points out all its weaknesses. He ignores our Constitution which has guided our freedom for generations, since established by people of great character and wisdom in its beginning. Is his character really American? What are his ultimate power ambitions?

On the other side are those who propose Americans do what Americans have traditionally done as encouraged by our U.S. Constitution - to proclaim they really are Americans. That is: get educated, get a job, do something positive, honor their mothers and fathers, and defend America with every breath in their body. They offer hope that we still have a choice to proclaim the idealistic values of those who founded our country by their blood, sweat, and tears. Those ideals are led by the concept of - do something for yourself, your family, and your country.

What are the ultimate goals of the 'one' who strives to tear apart the America we understand? Is it to be the one-world leader we read about in an ancient book? Many parallels from that ancient book create questions about the ambitions of this man. These parallels are given, fictionally of course, in my new book, '666: Mark of the Beast.'

Briefly, for example: that ancient book describes the beast as one whose origin is in question, unknown, only as an 'A'Syrian.' We know someone like that, whose origin has been in question since he was elected to a high office. That ancient book also describes the beast as one who mocks the Bible. We also know someone who accuses people of 'clinging to their guns and Bibles.' Is that not 'mocking the Bible?'

Based on the research for my book, I have been invited to be the guest speaker at the local Act4America meeting on June 5th. The signs from that ancient book grow stronger.

# 98

# Just Say It!

For over six months (now much longer) it seems like six years - the Democrats have been tossing around the theme 'fair share.' They claim the top 1-percent or some number, maybe those who make over $250,000 a year should pay more taxes, to pay their fair share. Then they claim they are not promoting 'class warfare' to divide our great country. I say their leaders' design is to divide and destroy our great country.

During all their class warfare rhetoric they have never suggested what a fair share should be. Until they cite a specific number, a dollar value or a percentage value, they are merely spouting rhetoric, which can be interpreted no other way than class warfare.

Currently, everyone who pays taxes pays what society, the government, requires. Since most of us believe we have a fair society, then everyone is paying his or her fair share. Those who try to cheat, or make an honest mistake, are ordinarily questioned by the IRS. Until the law changes, everyone is paying their fair share - legally, morally, and socially. Personally, I believe every American who respects and loves our country should pay at least one dollar in taxes. No one should get a free ride in a country as great as ours.

Now back to the grand design for their class warfare. Certainly, it's planned to weaken and subjugate America. A divided nation, culture, family, or friendship, cannot endure. Clearly, Obama wants to make America similar to that of the land of his father's - a pitiful country. That way he can be king, emperor, president for life, or whatever he decides to proclaim himself.

It's time those who proclaim the more successful people among us should pay their 'fair share' should put up or shut up. They should be pinned to the wall to say how much that should be. If they can't answer that question, then they have no argument. It means their only aim is to divide our society so it can fail. It's also time the conservatives have enough guts to pin them to the wall every time they use this divisive phrase. Have enough guts to challenge them for a specific number or percentage. Wake up! Do your duty!

# 99

# Why Allow Infiltration?

Much discussion lately centers around the idea and the possibility that Iranian terrorists are infiltrating through our southern borders, especially Arizona. Last year even an Islamic Jihad instruction booklet was found on the Arizona border near Casa Grande. For those who are not familiar with that area, it's at the intersection of Interstates 8 and 10, not far from Tucson and Phoenix.

Furthermore, according to those discussions and more revelations, the Jihadists have joined drug cartels in a combined effort to infiltrate the borders even more aggressively. Why would drug kingpins allow foreign terrorists to join them in their objectives? During 2010, I wrote a novel, America 20XX: The New World Order, that I published in January, 2011. During 2009, while driving through that area on my way to visit my children and grandchildren in California, the idea captured my thoughts that this would be the most likely area we would be invaded, by sneaky infiltration. That's why I started the book. Alas, it has become true. The location is perfect, especially night infiltration, with experienced guides. They are doing exactly what my book revealed - fictionally, of course.

Unfortunately, many people are found dead on those trails. And, many of those dead people have been shot - murdered. Why are they murdered? The dominant reason given is for money, or false promises by those 'mules.' To me, it's also logical there's another reason; discovery of infiltrating Jihadists by people who would jeopardize their sneaky infiltration. If they know what's happening and don't agree with it, they are murdered.

My question, and the reason for the book, is to ask: why isn't our president and his administration not interested in stopping that infiltration, and closing that border? Why do they hamper local immigration enforcement, and charge those who try to stop this invasion with crimes? What is the real intent of the president? Arizona is rightfully fighting for self-preservation.

My book fictionally answers many of these questions, including where the terrorist activity will begin, how, and why. I believe Phoenix should be on active alert, at all times.

# 100

# Confusion

Have you ever wondered why there is so much confusion concerning the direction in which our great country, America, is going or moving or changing? I had that same question the past three years, which is the major purpose for my writings. Researching deeply for several months I reached the conclusion that our traditional American way of life, the one on which our Constitution and culture was founded, is being attacked from two directions - not just one. One: The radical Islamists are trying to gain power over the world and must demonstrate their power by attacking America. Two: American Socialists are determined to change our economic system, which includes our American values and culture.

Radical Islamists have nothing to lose by continuing to attack values and beliefs not controlled by their dogma. Their total focus is only on their religion and their ideology. That ideology is so ingrained and fundamental that logic and reason will never change that. It has been their focus for hundreds of years. Their greatest weapon is terrorism and fear - we have changed our way of life and our natural freedoms in response to that fear. Perhaps if we focused less on political correctness, we could return to our American historical strength of,

'Enough is Enough, Don't Tread on Me.' We should make them fear even thinking about attacking us. Any other way continues to demonstrate our fear and weakness.

Obama is becoming more and more out front in his leadership of the Socialism movement. His pronouncement and leadership in the 'class warfare' movement is becoming even more blatant in his obvious attempt to 'spread the wealth around.' He makes no mention to encourage people to participate in the Capitalist economic system by preparing themselves through education and effort to earn part of that wealth. He often uses the term 'economic justice' which brings his Socialist plan out in the open. During the MLK celebration another more Socialist term was introduced and supported by the president. It was 'distributive justice.' What on earth could that mean other than pure Socialism?

As you listen to the news, please keep these two concepts in mind. We are being attacked from two fronts, not just one.

# 101

## Obama's Goal

Our president seems very elated that Egypt and Libya have fallen and now search for new leadership. It is with great glee that he announces his military successes to bring these tyrants down.

Of course those leaders were tyrants - but what's new for that part of the world? Those countries have been led by tyrants, some even more extreme, for centuries. At least those tyrannical leaders posed no serious threat to the security of the United States or Israel.

Ronald Reagan taught Gaddafi not to tread on the U.S. Mubarak was getting too much money from the U.S. to cause or promote a security problem for us or for Israel. Now, the president is promoting the downfall of the Syrian leader, who poses no direct threat to our security. He also has demonstrated he has no positive interest in Israel.

America's influence is already waning in Iraq and Afghanistan. With all our billions spent there, and all the sacrifices of our dedicated military people, most likely they will yield to cultural pressure to be like the others in that region. Will it be a surprise when all Muslim countries in that region become linked under one charter, or one mission, with Iran being the leading force? Even Turkey is now leaning toward idealism of its neighbors.

Iran was once known as Persia. Remember how dogmatic Persia was in trying to expand their empire? Remember the 300 Spartans? None of their dogmatic idealism has changed. Yet, our president reaches out his hand to embrace them - after he bows to their Muslim king. The only people most likely to shake his hand are the leaders of the Muslim Brotherhood who will thank him for making their mission of uniting all radical Muslims throughout that region possible.

What is our president's goal? Is it to defend the U.S. Constitution and American citizens, as is his primary charter? Or, is it to facilitate the more rapid expansion of radical Islam throughout the world?

# CONCLUSION

The president of the United States has always been elected with the presumption that he will be the president of all the people of the United States. Barack Obama has shown that he has been the extreme exception to that expectation.

His first action was to divide the citizenry by blaming the successful for the misfortune of the unsuccessful, the poor. And, to reinforce that principle he continues his war on the more successful in his ambition to gain more power from those he uses to climb for even more power. These should be considered his doles, since he promises them a dole. This is similar to the idea of the proles described by George Orwell in his Big Brother book, '1984.'

But, why does he strive for more power and control? What is his ambition, other than that for which he was elected - to be president of all the people of the United States of America? His actions demonstrate that he has become oblivious to that elected responsibility.

Of course, no one other than himself can predict what his plans are, or even his ultimate goals. But at this time, his goals do not seem directed in the best and highest interests of the United States.

God bless America.

King Obama Blogs

## About the Author

Will Clark's author experiences began by writing inspection and evaluation reports in the U.S. Air Force. He is a retired Air Force officer and a Vietnam veteran, serving in Saigon from 1966 to 1967. His other overseas assignments include Misawa, Japan and Ankara, Turkey.

In 1995, he authored a book, 'How to Learn,' as a county-wide study skills project to encourage students to improve their grades in DeSoto County, Mississippi. Education supporters printed and distributed four thousand copies. He also wrote a weekly education column for a local newspaper, The Desoto County Tribune.

His next published book was 'School Bells and Broken Tales,' a parody of nursery rhyme characters, also a motivation and education book for children. His other books include 'Shades of Retribution,' a historical novel, and 'Simply Success,' a motivation guide for students and employees.

His action novels include a trilogy based on Atlantis and crystals. The first book is titled: 'The Atlantis Crystal.' The second book is titled: 'She Waits In Atlantis.' The third is: 'Return to Atlantis.' This trilogy is based on his travels while assigned to Turkey, site of the ancient city of Troy. While in Turkey, he visited the ruins of Troy and the seven biblical churches described in the Bible Book of Revelation.

His last novel, '666: Mark of the Beast,' is a sequel to his previous book, 'America 20XX: The New World Order.'

Clark and his wife, Marie, live in Diamondhead, Mississippi, where they play golf with many friends.

# King Obama Blogs

Related Books by the Author


AMERICA 20XX:
THE NEW WORLD ORDER

Synopsis

Vision is the new federal constabulary force established by U.S. President Arabar when funding is not available for states and municipalities to fund their own police and security forces. This major funding crisis results from the continuing rise in oil prices. Oil prices are controlled by an Islamic king, King Rayeed, determined to execute a successful jihad in America. He knows he must destroy America's strength before he can attack his final target, Israel.

President Arabar, conspiring with King Rayeed, refuses to use American resources to avert the crisis. Pretending to increase development of ethanol to counter that crisis, Arabar creates a food shortage crisis.

Vision increases its numbers by using jihadists smuggled into the United States through the porous Texas and Arizona borders. Their first act is to confiscate registered weapons from gun owners. Then they plan to rush in more Vision troops by ship to expand control. They are free to act as security forces because President Arabar has ordered our military forces to stand down and be prepared to guard against a foreign aerial attack.

The Texas governor, cooperating with Arizona Governor Ann Melody, enlists the help of his good friend, a retired Marine named Carl Brannan, to slow the invasion. Brannan forms a network of old friends throughout America to defeat the invasion. Their first goal is to thwart Vision's efforts to confiscate personal weapons. They do this by giving receipts for the weapons using Vision's receipt documents. Brannan and his three partners continue to harass Vision departments and installations, giving hope to others that someone is resisting the jihad.

Eventually, Brannan and his group are captured. To quell all resistance, President Arabar plans their public hanging in the National Mall. He is pleased when a million citizens show up to witness the event. Just before the levers are pulled, a million citizens point their weapons at Arabar and the hundred jihadists guarding the event.

Given the option of facing charges of treason or exiling himself to another country, Arabar chooses exile to King Rayeed's country. When he arrives, he gets the same homecoming as Saddam Hussein's sons-in-law. Before he left the United States he signed documents contrary to Islamic principles and beliefs.

Governor Ann Melody is elected president to reestablish a government based on the U.S. Constitution. John Marker, the Texas Governor, returns to Texas, to his favorite fishing hole.

## 666: MARK OF THE BEAST

## Synopsis

This story depicts a scenario of how and why the Battle of Armageddon might evolve in the near future. Although fictional, it incorporates current events and international relationships to show this evil and evolving situation. It begins with the question: Who is most likely to initiate that apocalyptic battle against Israel? That answer is simple, by considering who wants to destroy Israel at this very moment. It's the radical Islamic nations. They will stop at nothing to destroy Israel.

The leader of that battle will be the one-world leader at that time. This means the one-world leader must be a Muslim or a Muslim supporter. Muslims might even consider him their Messiah, while he pretends to be the other Messiah. That leader is described in the Bible as the 'Deceiver.'

When his reign begins he will be lauded as a 'man of peace' and will be respected and revered by all nations. His power will begin by becoming leader of the ten European nations (the countries of the north) that once were part of the Roman Empire.

Through treaties, sanctions, and threats, he will disarm countries and make them vulnerable to his real plans of destruction. He will also initiate his 'mark' to allow people to transact business. Without his mark, people will not be allowed to buy or sell items. The mark will be an interactive computer chip that will identify each person as a follower of the one-world leader. Once he has computer control over every person, he will evolve into the 'Beast' and begin his inhuman acts against humanity.

This book considers three situations. First, citizens must decide if they want to accept the Beast's mark so they can continue to live normally. They ask how can they live like humans if they can't buy or sell anything. Second, if they refuse the mark how can they survive, especially when the Beast's enforcers are trying to track them down and kill them. The Beast is enforcing his condition of 'homogeneity' whereby the population must be controlled within acceptable environmental factors. Third, the Beast must destroy America's strength to allow his final attack on Israel. What will happen to Israel? What will happen to America? The deadly Battle of Armageddon is the final scene in the book.

Other Books by the Author

Novels:
Shades of Retribution
The Atlantis Crystal
She Waits in Atlantis
Return to Atlantis

Children's Books
Forest Trails and Fairy Tales
Wishing Wells and Broken Tales
Student Study Skills
American Heroes: Students Who Learn

Non-Fiction:
Simply Success
The Education Jungle
How to Learn
The Day America Died
Obama's Ring: The Seat of Satan
Managing Without Conflict
The Peer Pressure Monster
King Obama: America's Greatest Danger